WHAT PSYCHOLOGY SAYS ABOUT RELIGION

What Psychology Says About Religion

by

WAYNE E. OATES

ASSOCIATION PRESS • New York

WHAT PSYCHOLOGY SAYS ABOUT RELIGION

Association Press, 291 Broadway,
New York 7, N. Y.

Price, 50 cents

Library of Congress catalog card number:
58-11533

Printed in the United States of America

PREFACE

These words are addressed to lay people concerning what psychology says about religion. The professional reader will bear this in mind. The dangers of oversimplification and overgeneralization have been ever-present, but have been overcome at least inasmuch as the short scope of these few pages will permit. Although I have not purposed to write to a professional audience, I have felt keenly the responsibility of representing psychologists in such a way that they will not seem to be misused. Yet, at the same time I have borne in mind the fact that psychology is such a widely diverse field that any hope I may have entertained of making *all* professional readers happy would have prevented the writing of the first line. Nevertheless, the conversation stimulated even by healthy disagreement, I could hope, will lead to a deeper consideration of psychology by the lay reader and a scientific interest in religion by the psychologist. If I accomplish this, my purpose will have been fulfilled.

The difficulty of this task has been further

complicated by the fact that what psychologists have had to say about religion has been, as is the case of any professional person except a minister, avocational rather than vocational. Their comments on religion are not usually a part of their systematic psychological formulations, but have been wrought, as they should have been, out of their more personal experiences. Consequently, the sources consulted may seem to have been hand picked for the author's own purposes, when in reality they were the main sources in which the subject at hand was discussed, whereas other authors tended to be silent.

The main focus of these pages, however, is to communicate meaningfully to the person untrained in psychology who, nevertheless, finds himself confronted with discussions among his friends and relatives, fellow church members and business associates on "what psychology says about religion." After having said to this person what follows here, I have listed a selected bibliography that will take him into the deeper complexities of the subject.

WAYNE E. OATES
Louisville, Kentucky

CONTENTS

Chapter 1

WHAT IS PSYCHOLOGY?

The word "psychology" is a much used and often misused word. It covers a multitude of popular misconceptions, pseudoscientific ideas, and scientific hypotheses concerning human life and experience. Any clear understanding of what psychology says about religion calls for a clarification of the popular misconceptions of psychology and an appreciation of what psychology really is.

Popular Misconceptions of Psychology

Psychology as magic. Have you ever noticed the avid interest that appears when the subject of hypnosis arises? Often hypnosis is foolishly used as a magician's parlor trick when it should never be used apart from medical supervision. In exactly this way, however, many people conceive of psychology as a kit bag of magic tricks to play on people. Immediately we must reject this as a popular misuse and misunderstanding of psychology. One of the most vivid examples of this kind of magical thinking about it appears when some persons go to a psychologist for counseling help. They think of him as a person who has a magical word to give them in an *ipse dixit* fashion which will be like a fairy wand waved over their troubles. Such "word magic" is expected. Yet the psychologist's skill in counseling requires time and patience in getting to know the client as a person in a durably established and faithfully carried-through relationship. His helpfulness comes through the cumulative effect of interview after interview. He works with the counselee in removing hindrances to personal growth and deep blind spots to the changes that need to be taking place in his life if he is to become the person that his potentiality indicates. This comes not through magic but through discipline, patience, and courage.

Psychology as manipulation of people. A mother is asked: "How did you get Johnny to take his nap?" She replies: "I used a little psychology on him." A pastor is complimented by his secretary for his "ability to maneuver people into doing what he wants them to do. Before they know it, they are eating out of his hand," she says. Many people consider this kind of sleight of hand as "psychology." They would, if pressed, define psychology as a way of making people do what you want them to do without letting them know it. Admittedly, American advertising has taken the hard-earned gains of psychology and psychiatry and converted them into "hidden persuaders." Admittedly, propagandists of every brand have "used" psychological warfare as a method of "forced indoctrination," "brain washing," and covert manipulation of men's minds. But the psychologists who are dedicated to their science as a science and not as a means for ulterior and unscientific ends say that this is a violation of all that they stand for. It turns persons into things, and this should never be done; for as Carl Rogers, one of the truly great psychologists of our time, says:

> . . . the relationship between a psychologist and a client is "a relationship between two persons, meeting at a deep and significant level, not between a person and a complex object." * [1]

* All footnotes and documentations are found under "Notes by Chapters" at the end of the book.

Psychology as clairvoyance. A clairvoyant is somebody who is supposed to be able to "see through" other people and to "discern" the course of human events in some special, hidden sort of way. Many people popularly think of psychology as clairvoyance, as a sort of "*spy*-chology." The psychologist is half-jokingly called a "mind reader," one who can tell what you are thinking whether you are thinking or not! This misconception has been aided and abetted by many immature and/or pseudo psychologists who, as Martin Buber has said, "treat the whole human being" as a collection of parts that obscure each other and therefore need "unmasking," "unveiling," or "taking apart."

Contrary to such misconceptions, the psychologist is subject to the same laws of "getting to know" a person in order to understand and appreciate that person as is anyone else. He is concerned with scientifically observing, defining, systematizing, and bringing himself under subjection to these laws. He is also concerned with teaching these laws to other people and not with keeping them as some mumbo jumbo secret of his own. The true psychologist is more often a teacher than not, and is committed to the teaching of the tested and demonstrated principles of life rather than to the practice of occult arts and black magic.

Psychology as a unified, commonly agreed-upon science. One of the most misleading assumptions about psychology today is portrayed in the saying, "Psychology tells us. . . ." The fallacy implicit in these words suggests that psychology as such is a commonly agreed-upon voice, one which we can quote with the same authority we use when we say: "Astronomers tell us that the earth is round and that the sun comes up on the east each morning."

When we come to ask "what psychology says about religion," this is the misconception we need most vigorously to resist and keep clearly before us. For instance, we can accurately say that some psychologists reject the validity of religious experience. We are then in the position, however, of saying, "Which psychologists?" After we have answered this question, we must go on to ask another question, "Do they reject the validity of religious experience by reason of their data as psychologists through the use of the methods of psychology and on the basis of definable psychological studies of religious experience? Or, do they reject religion for their own personal reasons as human beings and would they do so even if they were not psychologists?" These are important distinctions to make when we begin to make "broadside" statements concerning "what psychology says about religion." Psychologists have a wide variety of interpretations of religion, as we shall see.

This particular misconception of psychology calls to attention several "sandtraps" into which discussions such as we are engaging here get "bogged down." For instance, when we hear *a* psychologist say something commendatory or derogatory of religion, we jump to the conclusion that *all* psychologists would say the same thing. Furthermore, when we hear him say that *in some instances* religion is an infantile over-dependence of a person on his parents, we leap to the surmise that *all* psychologists believe that *everybody's* religion is *always* this way. Quite often the psychologists themselves make this kind of leap of surmise, generalizing about religion on the basis of casual observations and not on the basis of careful scientific research on the subject. But we ourselves must carefully avoid either misinterpreting them or letting ourselves fall with some of them into the sandtraps of overgeneralization.

A Clearer Understanding of Psychology

Psychology: a young science. Kurt Lewin, one of the most discerning of modern psychologists, has accurately said that psychology must be thought of as a young science. The first scientific psychological laboratory was established by Wilhelm Wundt in Leipzig, Germany, in 1879. The American Psychological Association was organized in 1892. As a science then, the field of psychology is just a little more than a half century old. In some areas of the science, the field has become more "exact" than in others. The psychology of sensation and perception–in other words, the study of the five senses and of the patterns of meaning derived from them– has become more experimentally exact.

Such areas as the psychology of personality, however, move on less exact and more hypothetical bases of research. Working hypotheses concerning "theoretical models" of personality are developed by the psychologist. He seeks to construct a pattern of concepts which is equally applicable to the facts of all areas of psychology. But in doing so, he makes no more assumptions than are necessary and seeks to revise his concepts on the basis of new facts which he discovers. As Lewin says, "in investigations of this kind [the psychologist] must deal with persons as wholes to a much greater extent than in the psychology of sensation." [2] This latter kind of psychology is much more relevant to and conversant with the religious concerns of mankind —that is, to quote Lewin again, "the individual's ideals, ambitions, and his social relationships."

Psychology: art and science. From what has been said, psychology must be understood as both an art and a science. It may be compared to the work of an artist. The laws of color, light and shade, dimensions of a work of art, and the like are exact. However, the work of the artist requires more of him than this. He must have a creative imagination, the capacity to interpret the wholeness of life through his artistic insight and understanding. The art and the science of the psychologist are to each other as the intake and the outlet of the body's heart action. Without the one you do not have the other. The relationship is much like the knowledge and the experience of the religious person. The Christian needs to know the facts of the Bible and of Christian history, but he can know all these without being a Christian. Being a Christian is far more than having a head full of biblical facts. Being a psychologist also is far more than merely mastering the experimentally demonstrated facts of the field of psychology. It demands the deep creative insight and understanding of life characteristic of the poet, the philosopher, and the prophet. And at just the point of these demands the psychologist begins to say something that is highly significant for religion. Here the psychologist becomes an interpreter of human life as well as one who describes what he sees.

Psychology: a method of observation and research. The psychologist, like any other scientist, is committed to the scientific method of observation of the events of human behavior, recording the results of his observations, and discovering causal interrelationships between the events he observes. Some areas of human experience, such as sensitivity to pain, light, sound, tastes, and odors, are more readily accessible to observation than others, such as deciding, changing one's mind, feeling guilty, and worshiping. Naturally the former can be more "objective" than the latter for, at the very best, the psychologist, particularly when he begins to draw conclusions about the more intangible aspects of human life, knows that his observation is but a "participant observation." Harry Stack Sullivan, one of the most influential of American psychiatrists, devised this concept of participant observation.[3] By it he means that the psychologist himself participates in creating the behavior which he is observing in the other person. He is involved in a relationship to the person which in itself must be entered as a part of the expert's observation.

Therefore, psychology as a science has been concerned not only with *objective* observations, but also with *introspection.* Introspection is a *subjective* method of observation, and much of psychological research consists of the psychologist's observations of his own reactions. An example of this is Sigmund Freud's *Interpretation of Dreams*,[4] in which he records, observes, and interprets many of his own dreams as well as those of his patients.

Consequently, when we ask what psychology has to say about religion, we want to know whether or not what it says is based upon careful observation and faithful obedience to the disciplines of research. At the same time, we want to know in what way the psychologist himself is involved "participantly" in his observations and conclusions concerning religion. Otherwise, his opinions and words about religion spring, not from his work *as a psychologist* but from his own personal disposition toward life. As such they are important, but no more important nor to be given any more weight than the opinion of any other person who is not a psychologist.

Psychology: a many-sided science. You may be ready to say: "But it is too much to expect a psychologist to apply his science to religion closely enough to have something to say which meets the standards of his function as a scientist."

To the contrary, it can be positively said that religious experience is *one* of the many areas of human experience in which careful scientific labor has been done by the many-sided, richly varied science of psychology. These studies will be the stuff of which the rest of this book is made. Not nearly so much work has been done on the scientific study of religion as needs to be done. However, what has been done has become influential out of all proportion to the amount of work behind it.

But suffice it to say here that psychology is a many-sided science, and religion is only one of the many areas to which it has been applied. A quick glance at the most authoritative compendium of psychology references, *The Psychological Abstracts*, reveals the extent of these areas. General psychology, physiological psychology, developmental psychology, social psychology, clinical psychology, guidance counseling, educational psychology, personnel psychology, industrial psychology, psychology of religion, and military psychology are only a few of the varieties of psychology which could be named.

The diversity of these fields of interest in itself re-emphasizes the earlier thought that psychology does not speak with a common voice nearly so often as the sophomore taking his first course would have us think. The objectives of the various kinds of psychologists cause them to arrive at varied conclusions. The experimental psychologist who perceives himself as a "pure" scientist is likely to call the psychologist of personality a philosopher, and not a psychologist at all. The psychologist of personality is likely in turn to call the experimentalist a biologist or a physiologist and not a psychologist at all. Both of these may feel ill at home with the medically trained psychiatrist whose primary concern is the therapy of mentally sick persons.

The clinical psychologist of today stands in between experimental and medical approaches to psychology. He is something of a mediator, bound in a real way to the exactness of method which characterizes the experimental psychologist as well as to the concern for persons which the psychiatrist has for his patient. Consequently the clinical psychologist is making an increasingly greater contribution to the understanding of religion. We may well look to him for more refined methods of studying religious experience. The objectives and methods of all these varieties of psychology seem to be converging upon each other more than formerly. They are bringing forth research material and conceptual hypotheses that are both relevant to and significant for the religious interpretation of life. Some of them have more to say at this point than others, and a few of them, as we shall see, maintain a discreet silence on the whole subject.

Psychology: a specific body of knowledge. Whereas the science of psychology is a young, many-sided science and whereas it does not speak with a commonly agreed-upon voice by any means, nevertheless psychologists have unearthed a specific body of knowledge. Likewise, their most-used hypotheses have become a part of our culture and affect our religious interpretation of life in many and vital ways. For instance, the data of psychologists in the fields of sensation and perception have become specific and agreed-upon facts, used by applied sciences to the great benefit of mankind. Take for example the benefit that has come to us in the study of sight, the correction of defects of vision, and so on. Or, take for instance the way in which the concept of the conscious and unconscious has become common coin in the thought-patterns of our day. The discussions of mental mechanisms such as rationalization, repression, and compensatory thinking, have become so much a part of our interpretations of life that we cannot reject these concepts without calling upon them to help us with our arguments against them! Psychology as both an art and a science is a vivid part of the warp and woof of today's culture and of the fabric of man's view of himself as a religious person. Therefore, the imperative need to know "what psychology says about religion" becomes manifest. But first we need to know wherein psychology is silent, wherein it has nothing to say about religion.

Chapter 2

WHERE PSYCHOLOGY IS SILENT ABOUT RELIGION

Some types of psychology, by their very nature, are speechless about religion. This may be because the particular psychology is so strictly defined that anything outside its very small orbit is considered to be irrelevant. Or, this speechlessness may grow out of the fact that the given type of psychology is so completely restricted to one area of application that all other areas of application are excluded.

For example, psychology may be so strictly defined in several ways that it has nothing to say about religion. When psychology makes a firm bid as an "exact science" such as physics or chemistry, it has thereby circumscribed the area of its concern. Such a psychology was evident in the early years of scientific psychology in the work of Wilhelm Wundt, E. B. Titchener, and others. They restricted their experiments to the study of sensation, image, and perception. They developed highly ingenious techniques of measuring the amount of stimulus necessary for stimulating the end organs of sensory experience. These devoted scientists made tremendous contributions. However, when one reads their research, he does not hear them saying anything about religion. He looks in vain for references to such problems as the nature of personality, the meaning of human guilt, the importance of acceptance and rejection, the development of personality. Earlier philosophical psychologists such as John Locke discussed sensation and perception, and along with it rejected the doctrine of innate ideas, thereby touching off a great theological discussion. Wilhelm Wundt wrote his massive treatments of folk psychology and ethics. But contemporary psychologists discuss religion separately. For instance, present-day psychologists show their interest in religion avocationally rather than vocationally. Religion has been spoken about by them apart from the discipline of psychology which they define so very strictly and rigidly as to exclude religion.

Furthermore, psychology may be so highly restricted to one area of application that any discussions of religion will be totally absent. For example, the study of animal psychology may only remotely and quite indirectly have any relevance at all for the field of religious experience. However, the psychologist may be profoundly dedicated to his task. His silence on the subject of religion when he speaks *as a psychologist* should not be interpreted as indifference, belligerence, sympathy, or any such feelings. Rather, it should be interpreted as the irrelevance of his psychology for religion.

The industrial psychologist may see his science as purely concerned with the time-and-motion stresses involved in the operation of industry. When asked what *his* psychology has to say about religion, the whole question may be one of which he has never thought at all. Or, take as another example the present psychological experiments in space medicine. The psychologist who devotes his life to the highly specialized problems that occur when a pilot is at "gravity zero" may be speechless when asked to comment on what psychology says about religion. The average person, not accustomed to the grueling necessities of highly specialized research, has difficulty imagining the way in which these disciplines exclude every other object of attention except the research area being studied.

Even though some types of psychology by their very nature are silent about religion, genuine religious overtones nevertheless appear in the work of such psychologists. The humanitarian implications of the psychological findings about vision for blind persons can carry very deep and moving religious implications. Likewise, the personal discipline and dedication of psychologists of these highly defined sorts has a religious character in and of itself. Such psychologists are moved by kindred emotions to those of the genuinely religious person—awe, curiosity, wonder, a sense of the mysterious, and a profound respect for human personality. They are often filled with a reverence which many callously religious people could well emulate. Nevertheless, when we hear them speaking *as psychologists,* we do not hear them discussing religion.

Deeper and more personal reasons for the silence of such psychologists about religion need to be noted. Often psychologists, too, live compartmentalized lives. The secular education which brought them to their professional status as psychologists, particularly in America, frequently has *required* that their educators be silent on the subject of religion. Furthermore, the psychologist's education has been highly overspecialized in the area of statistics, measurements, physics, and physiology, and there may be a general absence of a basic education in the humanities which would include art and religion. The silence of psychology about religion is part and parcel of the whole educational philosophy of our schools. The separation of church and state has been legally interpreted in such a way as to muzzle any conversation about the religious implications of the subjects being studied. This applies to all subjects, and psychology is no exception.

But probing even more deeply than this, we must recognize that psychologists often are silent on the subject of religion because they themselves have never been exposed to religious teaching. They have been "the lost sheep of the house of Israel" and have been neglected—especially during the process of their education—by the churches. Contemporary Protestantism, particularly, has been slow to grasp its opportunity in the communication of the Christian gospel to the professional person. Protestants have often fallen into the tacit assumption that a psychologist, by the very reason of the fact that he is a psychologist, *therefore* will not be interested in religion. This is not necessarily so. In fact, this is a prejudgment which results from stereotyped thinking. Stereotyped thinking hinders clear understanding by making us "pigeonhole" people into popular classifications. For instance, we may assume that *all* Jews are rich, that *all* Negroes are lazy, that *all* Southerners hate Negroes, that *all* physicists have pointed beards and thick glasses, and that *all* psychologists reject religion. This is stereotyped thought. The only way to overcome the shabbiness in which such thought leaves our attitudes is to keep an open mind and form our own opinion of each psychologist as a person, on the basis of personal experience with him and not on the basis of cartoon caricatures and popular stereotypes of his profession.

Other psychologists may be silent on the subject of religion because they have been wrongly exposed to religion. As Paul Tillich says, "We all know the pain we suffer when we meet people who reject the Gospel, although they have no authority for rejecting it, or meet other people who are not able to make a genuine decision about it, since the Gospel was never properly communicated to them."[1] Many psychologists are silent on religion because of the misrepresentation of religion which they have experienced in their own spiritual odyssey. They may be like William Sumner, a pioneer sociologist, who is said to have placed his religion in the upper dresser drawer. Twenty years later, after he was educated, he came back to look for it, and it was gone! Part of this neglect may be due to the fact that the *kind* of religion to which they were exposed in the beginning was like salt that had lost its savor.

An example of this is the biography of Sigmund Freud. Ernest Jones says that Freud "grew up devoid of any belief in a God or Immortality, and does not appear ever to have felt any need of it." This exemplifies the Jew, cut loose from his orthodox rootage, growing up with no religious instruction at all. On the other hand, Freud was later harshly exposed to religion at its worst, in the hatred of Christians for Jews. Jones also tells the story of how Freud's father had been pushed around by a group of Christians and had had his clothes muddied by them. Freud felt that his father should have fought back. He felt like the son of Hamilcar, Hannibal, and swore to take vengeance as did Hannibal on the Romans.[2]

But more basic than any of these reasons for the psychologist's silence about religion is the fact that many of them do not want to alienate themselves from people of branches of religion other than the one with which they are associated. Nor do they want to alienate themselves from people who are fundamentally hostile to religion. This is a professional reason for being silent about religion. It is the one that we can most respect. These psychologists prefer to express their religion tacitly rather than to speak loudly and protestingly in its behalf.

For example, the profoundly religious psychologist in this country, says Robert McLeod, professor of psychology at Cornell University, "does not apprehend religion as a threat to his freedom as he might in some other countries; but he knows that to be labeled as 'religious' is to risk a loss of status among his professional colleagues." [3] This may not be because the professional colleagues are necessarily "irreligious." They may simply resent their colleague's "using" religion as a way of promoting his own popularity professionally. This is vividly apparent among psychiatrists who are tempted to get patients to come to them because of an appearance of religion. They prefer to get patients on the basis of their competence as doctors rather than for any "religious" advertisement they may get. Hence, they are likely not to let their "left hand know what their right hand does" when it comes to being "religious" before men. In our day of the heavy advertisement of "religion," this reason for the silence of psychologists can be marked and copied by the churchman.

Finally, let it be said that the literature of contemporary psychology is remarkably silent about the uniquely and distinctively Christian kind of religion. Rarely, if ever, do you find a psychologist discussing the characteristics of a Christian way of life which are commendable from the psychological point of view. This is particularly true of Protestants who are psychologists. However, the Catholic religion is different at this point. For instance, the Association of Catholic Psychologists is a very active organization and brings the specifically Catholic interpretation of psychology to bear upon the discussions of their profession in an open and unabashed manner.

Many devout Christians complain about this particular silence of psychologists about religion. We need to probe the reasons for this silence. In the first place, the psychologist, by reason of the demands of his science, must stretch every nerve to be scientific and "unbiased." Furthermore, the psychologist, when he addresses himself to the problem of religious experience and seeks to say anything about it, usually tries to define the common elements in all sound or healthy religion, apart from any particular religious group or doctrine. The end result, however, of this silence is a "leveling process" through which the qualitative differences between religious interpretations of life are obscured. Likewise, these differences are obscured by certain eagerness for the "practical" in which one is almost led to think that two diametrically opposed truths are equally valuable if they get the same results. This may or may not be true. Such an approach goes to seed when we hear people saying: "It doesn't matter what you believe just so you arrive at the right place and have your heart in the right place."

Another result of this silence on the part of psychologists about religion is evident in the secularization of religion itself by psychology. Here a residual kind of "common" religion is set forth. Religion is reduced to its least common denominator. All types of religious beliefs, regardless of the glaring inconsistencies between them are lumped together, or to use a technical word, "syncretized." This last result may be one of the causes of the allure of Oriental religions for many psychologists today. The Oriental religions, contrary to the fundamentals of the Christian faith, are syncretistic religions. One can be a Buddhist, a Confucian, and a Shintoist all at the same time, for instance. However, the Christian faith portrays the Christian God and Father of our Lord Jesus Christ as a unique God, who claims all the Christian's allegiance, and excludes participation in the worship of other gods. This is not to say, however, that the Christian is not all the more tempted to deify his own particular interpretation of the Christian faith. In so doing, he loses perspective as to the meaning of Christian redemption for all men everywhere. Much of the provincialism and shallowness of our understanding of the Gospel is effectively removed by the serious study of non-Christian religions. Only after we have taken these religions seriously enough to study them well does the uniqueness of the Christian faith emerge most clearly.

Psychology, therefore, at the points of its silence about religion, needs the clarifying insights of meaningful conversation with theology. The conversation between the two must be vigorous and challenging. The succeeding chapters of this book will deal with this conversation. Now we begin to discuss what psychology *does* say about religion, and particularly the way in which this is relevant to the Christian interpretation of life. However, one more concluding observation needs to be made here. The real cause of confusion in our attempts to understand what psychology says about religion lies just at the points at which psychology is or should be silent about religion. Psychologists who strictly define and/or overspecialize their application of psychology are tempted to speak *ex cathedra* about religion. An example of this is the professor in introductory psychology courses who makes "side remarks" about religion, leaving the impression on immature college students that he is speaking *for psychology* about religion. Similarly, a very devout Christian who is a psychologist may leave a "halo" of piety around his subject even though the area of his research has never extended beyond experiments with animals. As has been said before, we, therefore, need to be sure that a given psychologist is speaking about religion and is not merely expressing a personal bias. Otherwise, he may be a man who has mastered a very strictly defined and highly restricted area of life and has begun to speak as if he were an authority on everything in general.

Chapter 3

RELIGION: BONDAGE TO IDOLS OR FREEDOM FOR GROWTH?

When psychology really begins to speak clearly about religion, religion becomes an open question and not a closed issue. Just because a thing is *called* religious does not necessarily commend it as being valuable to a careful psychologist. The scientific spirit requires that even our most cherished conclusion be re-examined in the light of factual experience. The more insecure a person is in his religious faith, the more difficult this is for him to do. He may even be "running to psychology" to shore up the weak spots in his faith. Or, he may be unduly suspicious of psychology because of his insecurity. The psychologists stop and ask: "But what is the essential character of this religion?" When they do this, the first affirmation contemporary psychologists have made about religion is as follows: "Religion *can* be a form of idolatrous bondage for the human spirit, but it *may* be a way of freedom for the human spirit."

Religion as social control versus religion as a quest for freedom. Both psychologists and sociologists have brought religion and religious institutions to task for exercising rigorous control over human personality. In his book, *Folkways and Mores*, William Sumner traced the process whereby habits, conveniences, and customs become folkways handed down from generation to generation. Then these folkways are endowed with emotional feeling and security defenses on the part of groups of people. After a while they are attributed moral strength. Finally they become religious taboos, controlling people's lives without "rhyme or reason." Paul H. Landis has pointed out the ways in which religion functions as a means of social control, conserves values that have been brought over from the past, is fostered by conservative adults who have vested interests at stake, and thus fends off the necessity of social change. Liston Pope, dean of Yale Divinity School, reinforces this judgment when he says: "The churches have tended to pass from a dynamic force for social change to a static sanction of the change effected." [1] Talcott Parsons is much less moralistic than Pope, however, when he sympathetically says that it is impossible for the church or any other organization to "influence the lives of men, without all the implications of having taken responsibility for influencing them, that is, without being involved in the moral dilemmas of power." [2]

The most specific example of the negative effects of religion as a force of repression and control appears in Sigmund Freud's discussion of civilized sexual morality and modern nervousness. He deplores Western religious controls of the sexual behavior of people which are so rigid and unnatural that the sexual abilities of the individual are impaired, perverted, or neuroticized. He points out how creative energies of young people are frustrated, delayed, and perverted by false morality until they are irresponsibly expressed in such "otiose pastimes" as petting, masturbation, and homosexuality. He scores the social control of forms of religion and ethics which teach that the only permissible aim for sexual behavior is the procreation of children.[3]

Talcott Parsons more explicitly names the Catholic Church for introducing "structural strain" in society by claiming to control all matters of faith and morals and encroaching upon the freedom of the individual.[4] This particularly applies to the control exercised by the Catholic Church over the family, the procreation of children, and the choice of a mate.

However, the reflective and thoughtful religious person need not think of this as something new. The Hebrew prophets deplored the way that people filled their lands with idols and bowed down to the works of their own hands, "to what their own fingers had made."[5] The apostle Paul rebuked early Christians in Galatia for turning back again to the weak and beggarly elemental spirits whose slaves they wanted to be once more. He scored them for observing days, months, and seasons, and years, and feared that he had labored over them in vain. He told them that they were no longer slaves but children of God and that the purpose of God in Christ was to release them from bondage to blind idols. He encouraged them by saying, "For freedom Christ has set us free; stand fast therefore, and do not submit again to a yoke of slavery." [6]

In a sense then the comments of social psychologists about religion are prophetic. They have reminded us that religion should be not merely a form of social control, but a vital force for social change. Olin T. Binkley has, on the basis of historical evidence, conclusively shown that "religion is a significant factor in social change. . . . It produced prophetic personalities, men and women of ethical insight and good will who disturb the mores." [7]

When some of our contemporary psychologists deride religion as a form of bondage, we reply by seeking to restore religion as a quest for freedom to grow in the likeness of God. The role of religion as a thrust for freedom, as a way of rebellion, and as a bursting of the old wine skins of social control has only recently begun to be appreciated by psychologists. The growing child, for instance, may rebel against the spiritual shallowness, religious indifference, lack of integrity, and domineering attitudes of parents as surely as another child will rebel against the pious parent who threatens or punishes with religion in his attempts to control him. Rigidity of personality appears often in the parental attitudes of the militant atheist in the same way it appears in the domineering but devout religious person.

Religion as "escape from freedom" versus religion as "facing responsibility." Erich Fromm, in his provocative works, points out how religion may be an escapism from the demands of responsible freedom of the human spirit. Idolatry of the state, material success, or professional identity may for all practical purposes become a fearful escape from a responsible claim of individual freedom and of being a person in one's own right. Fromm says that from the beginning "human existence and freedom are inseparable. Man is confronted with the choice between different courses of action." Man is called to be a part of nature, and yet to transcend nature. He is constantly trying to subdue nature and become free "from" it. This is a long-drawn-out process, and its consummation thrusts the individual into a "growing isolation, insecurity." He faces "growing doubt concerning one's role in the universe, the meaning of one's life, and with all that a growing feeling of one's powerlessness and insignificance as an individual." He has achieved freedom "from" nature but has no sure guide as to what his freedom is "to." Fromm says that the disproportion between the amount of negative freedom and the positive realization of a freedom to responsible self-realization "has led . . . to a panicky flight from freedom into new ties or at least into complete indifference." [8]

Just at this point religion becomes intensely relevant to man's situation, according to Fromm. He says that the Reformation became a thrust of man for human freedom and autonomy.[9] However, he also feels that the Reformation produced another kind of bondage by its doctrines of the depravity of man, whereby man's feeling of loneliness and insignificance were enlarged and he once again was forced to seek his security in external authority. Nevertheless, the vitality of religion lies at the headsprings of man's quest for freedom and is constantly overrunning static authoritarian systems into which anxious and insecure people flee from their freedom.

Religion as authoritarianism versus religion as an affirmation of the autonomy of the soul. This raises one of the issues at which contemporary psychology has most often challenged religion: Does religion contribute to the weakening of human personality by its authoritarianism? Or, can religion be an affirmation of the autonomy of the soul before God? Once again Erich Fromm says that when man "becomes more independent, self-reliant, and critical," at the same time "he becomes more isolated, alone, and afraid." As he faces himself as a "completely separate entity" he experiences an "unbearable state of powerlessness and aloneness." Fromm says that man can take either of two paths which are open to him. He can "relate himself spontaneously to the world in love and work," or, "he can fall back, . . . give up his freedom, and . . . try to overcome his aloneness by eliminating the gap that has arisen between his individual self and the world." In this latter instance, as has been said, he may choose an authoritarian kind of religion as one of the ways of escaping his true freedom.[10]

What is authoritarian religion, according to Fromm? How does it contrast with the autonomous character of man's freedom? Authoritarian religion is a religion of power, in which love, freedom, justice, and the dignity of human personality are excluded. The cardinal virtue of this religion is obedience and submission, and the cardinal sin is disobedience and rebellion. Man in the authoritarian religion is a nonentity, called to despise himself.

Two responses to Erich Fromm's position are worth careful attention here. First, Fromm has reactivated the humanitarian character of prophetic religion in the tradition of the Age of the Enlightenment. This era of our spiritual heritage was in many senses a reaction against extreme Calvinism, which often emphasized the authority and sovereignty of God to the total neglect of the worth of man as made in the image of God. The philosophers of the enlightenment, in aggressive reaction, developed a theology which had a vital doctrine of man as its moving motive. Theology became anthropology-oriented. The authoritarianism of Calvinism was challenged in much the same way that Fromm challenges it. The independence and freedom of man was affirmed as he affirms it. A positive reconstruction of a humanistic religious orientation was set forth as he does.

Second, Boisen challenges Fromm's interpretation of the aims of religion as "the emancipation of the person from all authority and to recognize that he has nothing to rely upon except himself." [11] Boisen would say that authority in and of itself is not evil, nor is independence intrinsically good. Rather the aim of the religious life is to translate external authority into an internal sense of responsibility through the love of God to whom man "owes unreserved allegience." At this same point, Smiley Blanton points out that Fromm does not "seem to understand the impact upon American culture of the Judeo-Christian idea of a loving God and the influence of this loving God in curbing and modifying our aggressions." [12] And J. J. Honigmann aptly observes that Fromm does not adequately appreciate the fact that independence and freedom are culturally given values which live alongside other cultural demands. Religious concern arises most potently when we have to choose between these varying demands. That choice is a religious choice.[13]

This choice is actually faced by classical Calvinism which affirms that man is always enslaved in bondage to some finite authority until he has found freedom from all such idols in the worship of the Eternal God as sovereign beyond all lesser allegiances. For instance, the distortions of a man's relationship to his earthly father are clarified most vividly in the supremacy of his allegiance to his heavenly Father. Then, and then only, can he really "call no man father,"[14] as Jesus commanded. Making the decision between "becoming free" and "learning to be responsible," according to Rollo May and O. H. Mowrer, presents the individual with a real moral crisis. They both point out how many people "have guilt and anxiety because they have become 'autonomous' without having become 'responsible.'"[15]

Other psychologists have made constructive distinctions about the *kind* of religion which is ordinarily associated with authoritarianism. In fact, they have distinguished between irrational and rational authority, between religion that is concerned with the "externals and formalities of religion" and that which thrives upon religion's "inner, personal insights." The former kind of religion compromises for practical results to the neglect of deeper spiritual issues and, as T. W. Adorno and his associates describe it, is cluttered up with "conventions, taboos, social appearances, and is concerned about and submissive to 'what folks will say.' "[16]

But contemporary psychologists do not stop at this negative way station to truth. Although they have called our attention to the way in which religion can become external, authoritarian, and provincial, they go on to say that religion *can* be a healing affirmation of the autonomy of the human spirit. Such a religion would be opposed to "adjustment counseling" and aim at the birth of the creative uniqueness of each human being's contribution to life. It would be experiential and aimed at a growing understanding of man's nature and of the spiritual laws governing his existence.

The main thrust of the argument of Fromm, Mowrer, May, and Adorno is set hard against those kinds of religion which think of the Sabbath as being more important than man for whom the Sabbath was made. They reject those kinds of religion which look upon mankind as a means to ecclesiastical power rather than as the end of God's love and justice. At the risk of being classified among the atheists, Fromm and certain other modern psychologists would be always warning us of the temptation to make an idol of our particular interpretations of God. As Fromm again points out, this may lead to "a new form of idolatry." [17]

In this sense, modern psychology revives a vital theme of the Hebrew prophets and of the apostle Paul. Paul wrote to the Romans and warned them against the irresponsibility and self-destructiveness of allowing themselves to be ruled by their own self-centered desires. He exclaimed with horror that Roman Christians could "sin all the more that grace might abound." He talked to them of the new self they had realized in Christ, as the first fruit of the birth of a new life, the planting of the Lord, and the new freedom from the power of death through the covenant of Christ. On the other hand, he scored the Galatians for running back again into the yokes of bondage of the authoritarian Jewish ceremonial system. The writer of the Book of Hebrews portrays the life of faith as a "going out" from the safe confines of the imperfect ceremonial systems and a seeking, amid the freedom of "that which is not seen," a city whose builder and maker is God. The writer of Hebrews epitomizes this in the man of faith, Abraham, who "when he was called . . . went out, not knowing where he went." The Protestant principle of the Christian faith has always had at its core the inalienable freedom of the human spirit. It has progressively reaffirmed the autonomy of man as a total self before God. In this sense, the Protestant Christian is at home with the psychologists as he thrusts aside the "sun and umbrella" which would hide man's autonomous spirit from the fullest light of the truth of the Eternal.

Chapter 4

RELIGION: CHILDISHNESS OR A WAY TO MATURITY?

Probably one of the greatest contributions that contemporary psychology has made to our understanding of religion has been at the point of the detailed studies of the development of personality. The psychologist has helped us to see that religion, like the sunlight of each day, appears differently at each developmental stage of our growth. Psychologists have helped us to be much more specific in our evaluation of religious experience by giving us a better understanding of the "stages along life's way from birth to maturity." They have raised the question of the degree of childishness or maturity in any given religious expression. Therefore another affirmation of modern psychology about religion can be stated as follows: "Religion *can* be childish, but religion *may* be a way to maturity."

Religion as childishness or immaturity. Men

like Sören Kierkegaard and Horace Bushnell produced poetic and prophetic descriptions of the religious development of personality. Sören Kierkegaard (1813-1855), who saw himself at times as a psychologist wrote a profound psychological work entitled *The Sickness unto Death.*[1] In it he described the struggles of the soul as man seeks "to become a self" before God, the despair of never having attempted to become the self God intends for him to be, the despair of having attempted to become this self and failed, and the despair of having achieved that freedom and selfhood but yet not knowing how to bear the responsibility attendant upon it. Kierkegaard described the spiritual immaturity of the "aesthetic man," who had not come to grips with time, who was bound to the desires which compelled him to act without the freedom of reflection, and who was always looking for some new thing to save him from boredom. Kierkegaard poetically discerned the spiritual adolescence—regardless of chronological age—of the ethicist who has to have a rule for everything, lives in the hope of a legal and authoritarian structure which will release him from constant demand for decisions, and free him from the narrowing anxiety of choice. Kierkegaard penetrated the maturing character of the "leap of faith" in which law is translated into grace and the distorted perception of God as a destroyer is transformed into a relationship to God as Redemptive *Agape*, or Unconditional Love.

Horace Bushnell (1802-1876), although he held to the Calvinistic doctrine of the corruption of human nature, felt that the redemptive work of God should be begun at the earliest possible moment and that children should "grow up in love with all goodness, and remember no definite time when they became subject to the Christian principle." [2] Pursuant of this conviction, Bushnell began to apply a distinctly psychological criterion to the religious nurture of children. Through the theological breach which Bushnell opened, later psychological findings have been thrust. The moral value scale of childishness-maturity has, as a result, become a detailed part of our modern ethical norms in a way not known to previous eras of religious history.

Sigmund Freud initiated the development of one of the most often quoted hypotheses concerning the growth of a human person. In his book, *The Future of an Illusion*, he describes religion as a continuation of the child's need for protection in the presence of feelings of helplessness. He says that "when the child grows up and finds that he is destined to remain a child forever, and that he can never do without protection against unknown and mighty powers, he invests these with the traits of the father figure; he creates for himself the gods, of whom he is afraid, whom he seeks to propitiate, and to whom he nevertheless trusts the task of protecting him." Thus the "longing-for-the-father explanation" of religion as the child's defensive reaction to his helplessness "gives the characteristic features to the adult's reaction to his own helplessness, i.e., the formation of religion." [3] Then Freud chastises us for introducing a child to the "doctrines of religion at a time when he is neither interested in them nor capable of grasping their import." [4]

Yet, a less moralistic, more discerning evaluation of religion, the Christian religion in particular, is made by J. C. Flügel, another and more recent psychoanalyst, when he compares Christianity and psychoanalysis. He says that (1) "both aim at reducing guilt"; (2) in both there is a tendency to look upon suffering as punishment for infringing upon the command of some stern authority," either parents or God; (3) in both, this stern authority is "replaced by a mild, kindly, healing authority, with a view to eventual individual moral autonomy." He says that "Christianity is predominantly a son and brother religion and not a father religion," one based upon co-operative relationships between people rather than childish servility of weak persons upon stronger ones.[5]

Even more specifically than Flügel's remarks, another and more recent psychologist, Gordon W. Allport, professor of psychology at Harvard University, says that religion is not "a mere matter of dependency or of reliving the family or cultural configuration . . . any single formula by itself is too partial." Then he points out the many one-sided emphases in "psychological discussions of religion." He rightly observes that one reason for this is that personality development has been "much more thoroughly studied for the years preceding puberty than for adolescent and adult years." As a result we have psychologists who have developed a distorted view of religion in that they present religion as childishness and overemphasize in our present view those factors influencing the religion of childhood: "families, dependence, authority, wishful thinking, and magical practice."[6] Allport wisely contends that the process of becoming a person continues throughout life and cannot be explained on the basis of what happens before puberty. He points out that an adequate religious world view is not possible for children, and that one does not feel oneself "meaningfully linked to the whole Being . . . before puberty." The adult discovers that he needs faith and love, and "a comprehensive belief system capable of relating him to existence as a whole." [7] He points out that a man cannot live without "his own ultimate presuppositions." And these are for him "the forward intention" that make it possible for him "at each stage of his becoming to relate himself meaningfully to the totality of Being." In another book,[8] Allport says that religion may be a throwback to childhood, but it is often the central organizing factor in a human life, representing men's longest-range intentions, and capable of conferring marked integration upon personality, engendering meaning and peace in the face of tragedy and confusion of life.

More recently psychologists have concentrated

increased attention upon the adult years of life. As the main complexities of adulthood have become more accurately perceived, interestingly enough, psychology's evaluation of religion has shifted from the dark rejections of Freud to the more positive affirmations of Allport. As we shall see in the later chapter on religion as meaningfulness in life, the need for careful psychological studies of adulthood is imperative. Adulthood has become increasingly a time of meaninglessness in people's lives. For a sheer lack of purpose and sense of the worthwhileness of the mature years, many adults will regress to an earlier, more immature way of meeting life. Particularly is this true of their religion. During the self-sufficient years of their twenties, they will neglect to develop their religious understanding and spiritual resources. The goal structures of modern psychology have been aimed at getting a person *away* from childhood and not at clearly assessing the meanings and purpose of adult living. As a result of this lack, many psychological evaluations of religion stop at such negations as the charge of childishness, something to be "outgrown."

Religion as a way to maturity. When we face the distortions of religion characteristic of immature and neurotic as well as psychotic persons, we are forced to conclude that religion *may* be extremely childish. We nevertheless must include all the evidence and say that religion *can* be a way to maturity. In one of his case histories, Freud says that religion normally should "lower the importance of the early family" and "give the instinctual strivings of the growing child a safe mooring place" as well as "enable the adult to gain access in love to the larger family of mankind."

Harry Stack Sullivan defined maturity as the capacity "to establish relationships of love for some other person, in which relationship the other person is as significant, or nearly as significant, as oneself."[9] Gordon Allport, again, observes that the mature person goes on developing in depth and scope of interest until old age and that the "mature religious sentiment" is marked by comprehensiveness of affection, an awareness of one's own partial grasp of the love and knowledge of God, and "seems never satisfied, as it is dealing with matters central with all existence."[10] And, to point to another psychologist, Leon J. Saul says that "religion . . . represents in essence . . . man's . . . struggle between the animal impulses and the restraining socializing forces of parental authority. This is all a part of the struggle of mankind to grow up and live together civilly—an age-old struggle which is reflected in almost all human thought and endeavor from dreams to great organization."[11]

Religion, then, from a psychological point of view, may well be a way to maturity, that is, the capacity to love one's neighbor as himself. This does not mean that religion is *necessarily* a way to maturity. Neither does it mean that religion is *just* a means to maturity. The depths of religious experience are not exhausted by the psychological conception of maturity. Nor does the conception of maturity express all that psychology has to say about religion. But the claims of adulthood call for the resources of a mature faith.

We are particularly indebted to C. G. Jung for his insight into the role of religion in adulthood. His famous statement that he has never seen a patient beyond the age of thirty-five who was not suffering from a failure of faith is often quoted. However, it is rarely if ever pointed out that Jung is emphasizing religious faith as a normal part of the healthy adult's life, the life he has "beyond the age of thirty-five." Religion is not necessarily a "throwback" to childhood, but may well be the mature person's serious confrontation of the reality of adult living. Furthermore, the main thrust of Jung's teachings are concerned with the creative release of the deepest potentials of the individual as a member of the human race. This release comes through the individual's discovery of his vocation in life, his particular calling, his basic identity. The religious concern and spiritual faith of the maturing person center upon the discovery, formulation, enunciation, and social expression of this calling, according to Jung.

The concerned Christian who seriously examines the New Testament hears these sayings of modern psychology about religion, childishness, and maturity with a quaint sense of familiarity. He has heard this somewhere before. The New Testament speaks of maturity in Christ. This maturity is summed up in the thirteenth chapter of I Corinthians as the excellent gift of Christian love. It calls for putting away childish things for humility in the presence of the incompleteness of our prophecy, our understanding, our knowledge, and our faith. Growing up in love according to Ephesians 4:14-16, implies stability of personhood, rejection of deceptiveness, speaking the truth in love, and becoming co-ordinated with the fellowship of believers, the body of Christ, of which he is the head. The Book of Hebrews draws a sharp distinction between the childish "need of milk" on the part of immature Christians as compared with the mature use of strong meat by them "that are of full age, even those who by reason of use have their senses exercised to discern both good and evil." [12]

Whereas the contemporary psychologist has not given the Christian the criterion of maturity for evaluating his religion, nevertheless he has given us detailed empirical studies of personality growth and has enabled us to be more specific in our understanding of what maturity is. The developmental studies of Sigmund Freud, Harry Stack Sullivan, Arnold Gesell, Milton J. Senn, and others have enabled us to be much more precise in our evaluation of the stages of spiritual maturity in the light of the individual's capacity to love, to relate himself to other people, and to live with an increasingly "productive orientation" to life.

Furthermore, the more psychologists have faced up to an attempt to assess personality as a whole rather than simply to describe this or that function of the total person, the more they have become concerned about value judgments such as the concept of maturity is in itself. As Lawrence E. Cole points out, the psychologist, under these circumstances, "reveals *his* values," he reflects his own ethical perspective. The psychologist must move out of his relativisms and his attempt at neutrality in the realm of spiritual values and become a participant in the ethical strivings of the human race. Otherwise he is a mere technician, the results of whose technical work must be interpreted by other persons who are capable of the search for a comprehensive understanding of human life.

Chapter 5

RELIGION: A SICKNESS OR A WAY TO HEALTH?

Not all types of psychology are concerned with the problem of the therapy of sick people. However, as this concern has become more and more predominant, contemporary psychologists have widened the range of their interests and sought to develop a more comprehensive understanding of human life. This trend has been stimulated most by the medical psychologists and/or psychiatric profession. Mental illness is one of the major diseases of human life today. Psychologists and psychiatrists are intensively applying their findings to the problems of the mentally ill. This kind of research is poorly supported by public and private funds, even yet. But as research men have worked, some of them have been deeply impressed by the way in which religion enters mental illness and how religion can participate in the therapy of such disorders. Consequently, with the whole issue of religion an open question and not a settled conclusion with them, psychologists and psychiatrists have begun to frame another hypothesis about religion: "Religion *may* be a part of a mental sickness in and of itself, but it *can* be a way to health." This issue is such an intensely important one that I have given it extensive and detailed attention in my own book, *Religious Factors in Mental Illness.*[1] A more detailed treatment of this particular aspect of psychology and religion is found in that book.

Religion as a neurosis, or a disease, of mankind. Among the early and most blatant of the behavioristic psychologists was John B. Watson. He insisted that psychology is an exact science of human behavior. He was one of those academic psychologists who tried to imitate the natural sciences and laboratory methods of weighing and counting. He was one of those who urged that psychology become a science concerned with "mechanisms, reaction-formation, instincts, but not with the most specifically human phenomena: love, reason, conscience, values." He was one of the psychologists who "was more often concerned with insignificant problems than with devising new methods to study the significant problems of man." [2] Watson was dogmatically convinced that human behavior can be controlled and predicted with absolute exactness. Therefore, to him, religion was a thing of the past. He thought of religion as having arisen from "the general laziness of mankind" and as a fiction forced upon stupid people by priests. His more blatant remarks have been sloughed off by contemporary psychologists of the behavioristic school. But this fond hope that behavior may be predicted with absolute precision and controlled with finality still is a messianic hope of some psychologists. Suffice it to say here that Watson's general perspective was that religion is one of the degenerative barnacles on the side of the human race. Like a barnacle, religion should be knocked off. Like a disease it should be gotten over!

A much more carefully thought-out consideration of religion as a neurosis is found in a paper by Sigmund Freud entitled "Obsessive Acts and Religious Practices." [3] Freud observed the "ceremonial nature of neurotic behavior. The washing of hands and other compulsive rites of the mentally sick neurotic had all the stereotyped character of religious ritual. Freud thought of these obsessional neurotic practices as a tragic, comic travesty of a *private* religion. Instead of being communally agreed-upon practices of many people in relation to each other, they were the isolated, private, and lonely experiences of a sick person. Freud concluded that religion could "be compared to an individual obsessional neurosis. . . ." He said that the "true believer is in a high degree protected against the danger of certain neurotic afflictions." This protection is afforded him "by accepting the universal neurosis of religion." Freud said that when an individual accepts this universal neurosis "he is spared the task of forming a personal neurosis." Therefore, he thought of religious dogma as "neurotic survivals" which in time could be replaced by "the results of rational effort, as in the analytic treatment of neurotics." [4] Freud proposed that psychoanalytic therapy, on the other hand, when set forth on a universally accepted basis, would become the answer to this universal neurosis. Yet some of his closest students and most penetrating critics look upon this not as an invalidation of religion, but as a somewhat unconscious attempt of Freud to establish psychoanalysis as a rival religion!

Three observations need to be made here about Freud's trenchant criticisms of religion. First, as has been said before, psychology is a young science. Even casual observations of the history of science and religion have revealed that a young science is marked by its competition with religion. In a very real way science has secularized one area of religion after another, always pushing religion to a deeper analysis of its reason for being. The sciences of cosmology—astronomy, physics, geography, and so on—were originally the domain of religious interpretation. Medicine was the practice of the priesthood. Education was the sole prerogative of the church. Even sanitation was under the control of ceremonial laws of cleanness and uncleanness, dietary regimen, and the like. Through the processes of secularization one of these areas after another has been reassessed and taken over by some scientific discipline. In order to do this, a young science has to go through a "phase" of rejecting religion, and religion has to go through a phase of being "threatened" by the young science.

Both this rejecting attitude of the young science and the feelings of "threat" characteristic of religion tend to move into a new phase of security and conciliation after the young science has established its independence. Then the danger is to throw judgment to the wind and make the science and religion exactly the same thing although their presuppositions about life may be unexamined and really quite disparate from and opposed to each other.

Second, the particular criticism of religion as being a neurosis made by Freud was modified in another of his writings. In his book, *Civilization and Its Discontents*, he says that in his *Future of an Illusion* he was "concerned much less with the deepest sources of religious feeling than with what the ordinary man understands about his religion. . . ." He says that popular religion is "so patently infantile, so incongruous with reality, that to the one whose attitude to humanity is friendly it is painful to think that the great majority of mortals will never be able to rise above this view of life." [5] Yet, for Freud to admit that he was not talking about the deepest sources of religious feeling, is a tremendous concession.

This admission opens the way for asking psychoanalysts to explore with us precisely *what* these "deepest sources of religion" are, and to lay hold of the value of psychoanalytic studies in understanding these sources. Freud himself encouraged this.

The third observation about psychologists' assessment of religion as psychopathology would be to challenge the psychologists' research basis for this judgment. To take a mentally sick person's religion as a criterion of the nature and worth of religion is equivalent to saying that his reactions are to be the criterion of value in other areas also. To say this is to take the mentally sick person's evaluation of psychology and psychiatry as final. This would be absurd, because the psychologist's and psychiatrist's sciences are in low repute, particularly among mentally sick persons who often prefer their disease to its alternatives of responsibility and health. In turn, the lay person must be slow to take a neurotic or psychotic person's evaluation of psychology and psychiatry as valid. Therefore, religion greatly needs careful psychological studies of the productively oriented, responsibly related person's religious experience. Only then can the judgment of religion as a neurosis or disease be placed in proper perspective.

Religion as a way to health. Not all psychologists by any means agree with Sigmund Freud in his estimate of religion. Some of them have sought to evaluate the creative power of religion. An increasing number of competent psychologists and psychiatrists are considering the role of religion in the therapy of mentally disturbed people as a positive benefit. However, they build these considerations upon a careful distinction between the religion of the neurotic person and the religion of the mature person. For instance, Paul Bergman records the case of a patient who experienced a dynamic religious conversion in the course of psychotherapy. In the process of it his religious faith shifted from an external, fearful anxiety over authority to one of an internal, positive religious meaning. He laid hold of the more positive and loving aspects of his Christian tradition, especially in relation to a secure and serenely religious grandmother. Furthermore, he no longer needed to "take a drink" in order to solve his problems. Also, certain suicidal ideas of his underwent marked change. And finally his interpersonal relationships become more realistic and meaningful.[6]

Harry M. Tiebout has had unusually large amounts of experience in dealing with alcoholics. He says that religion can work creatively in the therapy of the alcoholic. As it releases "the positive potential which resides in the unconscious . . . it actually makes (the alcoholic) freer to meet life anew . . . he feels that he is in communion with God, man, and all the creative forces of the universe." [7]

Yet these psychologists are not making blanket judgments about "just any kind of religion." Leon Salzman, another psychiatrist, describes religious experience in and out of the course of therapy under two headings: "(1) Progressive or maturational type of religious experience, and (2) the regressive or psychopathological type of religious experience." The former type issues in "the positive fulfillment of one's powers with self-awareness, concern for others, and oneness with the world." There is conjunctive experience which lessens anxiety and integrates the mature development of the life of the person. The latter type, or the regressive of pathological experience, is a "pseudo-solution . . . brought about by increasing anxieties, and has a disjunctive effect on the personality." [8]

Alphonse Maeder, a Swiss psychiatrist, in his book, *Ways to Psychic Health*, looks upon religion as an indispensable part of the process of psychotherapy itself. He says that "psychological illumination and transformation are not sufficient. An ethical-religious purification is necessary; one must get to the core of things." [9] He continues by saying that "science does not encompass the entire reality of Man. Faith, however, remains as the central concern of the individual." The remainder of his book portrays the lively interaction between medical psychotherapy and pastoral care in the therapy of neurotic persons. Contrary to the optimistic view of man apparent in the teaching of Erich Fromm, Maeder sees man as "guilty before God," bound by sin, burdened by his need for confession. Through confession "the heavy burden falls away from him, he becomes free. It is as though he had been confined in a narrow dungeon and now the separating wall has fallen." [10] Also, Maeder interprets religious experience as free acceptance of "dependence upon and the leadership of God." Now, instead of being a closed, unteachable self, he becomes an open, learning self—a disciple.

In this chapter, again, the psychologists have had something important to say about religion. They have reaffirmed that which the prophets of the Hebrew-Christian faith sought to communicate to us, namely, that being "religious in all things" is not necessarily a virtue. They have underscored the necessity that we learn to "try the spirits" of religion to see whether they are real or counterfeit. The Hebrew-Christian faith has always distinguished between healthy and unhealthy religion by calling one idolatry and the other the worship of the true and living God. The blind and compulsive participation in the rituals of religion finds no more approval in the pages of the Old and New Testament than it does among modern psychologists. The main difference is that some modern psychologists feel themselves forced to be atheists when they reject the petty idolatries of popular superstitions. Whereas some of the enemies of Old and New Testament writers thought of them as being atheists and blasphemers, they felt themselves to be seeking after the living God. Contemporary psychologists say that much of present-day religion "has led to a new form of idolatry. An image of God, not in wood and stone but in words, is erected so that people would worship at this shrine." [11] Then, remarkably enough they quote Jesus and the prophets to substantiate their point of view! Then they ask, as Fromm does: "Are we still concerned with the problem of idolatry? . . . The essence of idolatry is a specific human attitude [that] . . . may be described as deification of things, of partial aspects of the world and man's submission to such things." [12]

A dark tragedy of our society mutely resides in the fact that intellectuals in considerable numbers cannot reject that which is unreal and fallacious in popular religion without feeling compelled to think of themselves as "atheists." Yet some of their more reflective statements strike more really at the true nature of the life of the spirit than possibly even they would be willing to concede. A part of this tragedy is due to the hard-driving propaganda of religionists who close the door of discernment and discussion in behalf of immediate decisions "for" or "against" religion as they see it. As a result "in-group" and "out-group" tensions prevent real communication except between those who speak the same "in-group" language and share the same emotional connotations attached to that language. There is some reason to think that this same process may go on also within professional groups such as psychologists. All this points both to the difficulty of and necessity for real effort on the part of the churches to communicate with the professional people, even apart from our objectives of increasing our membership. American churches have been swift to involve business people in the life and leadership of the working organization of the churches. But we have been slow, indifferent, suspicious, or even hostile toward drawing upon the resources of professional people. However, vigorous growth at this point is taking place, as is evident in the training of ministers to co-operate with other professional persons in pastoral care as well as to face the religious questions and scientific acumen with which these persons approach the whole issue of the religious life and needs of people.

Chapter 6

RELIGION: AN ILLUSION OR A WAY TO REALITY?

The capacity to discern the difference between an idol and the true and living God, between unreality and Reality, calls into account *man's ability to perceive reality, to see things as they are.* The psychologist brings the processes of perceiving into the laboratory. He asks questions about man's ability to evaluate what is real and to separate it from that which is unreal. Therefore, when psychologists begin to talk about religion, Professor Robert B. McLeod of Cornell reminds us, their task "is to distinguish between what is illusory and what is a true representation." [1] Religion still remains an open question to the psychologist in this respect also. The psychologist refuses to pass judgment on any kind of human behavior, especially religious behavior, before he has even looked at it. Therefore, another one of the "open-ended" hypotheses of contemporary psychology about religion is as follows: "Religion *may* be an illusion, but it *can* be a way to reality." Every student of perception knows how very difficult it is to draw a line between what is correctly and what is incorrectly perceived. Therefore, he may jump to the conclusion that all perception is illusion and that our values, particularly our religious values, are basically the "will to believe" anyhow and that we believe what we want to believe, regardless of fact or fantasy in perception.

Religion as an illusion. The main contribution of modern psychology has been to insist doggedly upon the distinctly personal dimensions of religious faith. Sören Kierkegaard accented this when he said that the truth that edifies, the one that is worth using the precious time of the given moment to contemplate, is the truth *for me.* In other words, the truth that has become truth in my own personal experience, appropriated inwardly by me, is the only truth that edifies me. The pietistic person says the same thing when he says that unless we have had a personal experience with Christ, we cannot grasp the meaning of the Bible. He is likely to go further and say that those parts of the Bible which are *his*, which he knows from personal experience to be true, are very different from those parts of the Bible which are not *his*, which he has not personally applied and appropriated. Friedrich Schleiermacher (1768-1834), one of the precursors of the psychological interpretation of religion, defined God in terms of the human self-consciousness of absolute dependence. God as "implied" in the "whence" of this feeling of dependence was the domain of speculation, but God as really existing was this self-consciousness of absolute dependence in man. Whereas these insistences of Kierkegaard and Schleiermacher produced an acute awareness of the personal dimensions of religious faith, they nevertheless raised serious questions whether God's existence were in any wise independent of man's existence, as to whether, if man were not, God would not be.

Ludwig Feuerbach (1804-1872) turned these serious questions into answers, to his own satisfaction, to say the least. He set himself to the task of turning "theology" into anthropology. For, he said, "Man is the beginning, the middle, and the end of religion." [2] Feuerbach felt that man, because he could not know God apart from his own consciousness, excused himself from the demands of "what is yet remaining of his religious conscience for his forgetfulness of God." [3] We misinterpret Feuerbach if we see in his teachings an attempt to reduce or explain away religion and theology. As Barth again says, "When he [Feuerbach] identifies God with the essence of man, he thereby pays God the highest honor he can confer." [4]

Exactly what Feuerbach does, is to equate God with the essence of man. He says that "the divine being is nothing else than the human being, or, rather, the human nature purified, freed from the limits of the individual man, made objective. . . ." [5] He then says, "I cannot know whether God is something else in himself or for himself than he is for me; what he is to me is all that he is. . . . The religious man finds perfect satisfaction in that which God is in relation to himself . . . for God is to him what he can alone be to man . . . but the distinction between object and conception—between God as he is in himself and God as he is for me—is a skeptical distinction, and therefore an irreligious one." [6]

With a deep sense of the personal dimensions of religion, therefore, Feuerbach set forth his idea of religion as "the dream of the human mind," the purpose of religion being self-knowledge. The "miraculous Redeemer is nothing else than the realized wish of feeling to be free from the laws of morality, . . . thus he becomes morally free and good through miracle." [7]

Nevertheless, the piety of Feuerbach did not hold true in the way modern psychologists rephrased his ideas in a purely skeptical context. For instance, we do not usually consider Karl Marx as a psychologist. Nevertheless, he contributed materially to the interpretation of religion as a psychological illusion. He said that "the religious world is but the reflex of the real world." He was sure that this "religious reflex" would "finally vanish" if and when life should offer "to man . . . perfectly intelligible and reasonable relations with regard to his fellow man and to nature." [8] For Marx, religion was an illusion which kept people happy on the hopes of an unreal world in the presence of shattered hopes and bitter disillusionments of a real world. Therefore religion is an "opiate" for easing the pain of a reality, a protection against things as they are.

Sigmund Freud also made his reputation concerning religion on his theory of religion as an illusion. He defined an illusion as a wish. In short, we wish for "protection against the consequences of human weakness" and therefore we project this wish onto a cosmic scheme and say that there is a God. Freud says that the religious illusion is one of the "oldest, strongest, and most insistent wishes of mankind," and that the strength of religion lies in "the strength of these wishes." [9] Like Feuerbach, Freud interpreted religion as the composite of the dreams of mankind. He declared that the intimately personal religion of the ordinary man was "the only religion that ought to bear the name." [10] However, Freud took the skeptical position that religion viewed the "real world" as "distorted like a delusion," which was an "intimidating influence upon intelligence." [11]

These challenging evaluations of religion by Freud and Marx stab directly at the heart of the religious person's relationship to reality. The whole problem of hope is at stake. Religion does consist, at least partially, of the hopes of mankind. Hebrews defines faith as the "substance of things hoped for, the evidence of things not seen."[12] Yet, Marx and Freud insist that unless one has realized his wishes and achieved his hopes, he is building his life on the basis of wish and hope. These are illusory and palliative.

Religion as a way to reality. This psychological evaluation of religion as an illusion has helped religion by negatively defining what God is not. Furthermore, psychologists have pushed us into a deeper analysis of man's capacity to know God. They have told us what we have already been told and should have known, namely, that our knowledge of God is but a "baffling reflection" which is "seen darkly" as if in a mirror. We know in part and we prophesy in part. We have often forgotten the partialness and distortion of our grasp of God's revelation in our efforts to extol the completeness of his action on our behalf in Christ. Psychologists have reminded us of this to our great benefit. In asking their help, however, we cannot go to unasked-for extremes and reject as invalid what we do know of God. Even though we are fully aware that we do not have a knowledge of God except that which comes to us through our selfhood and is conscious to us in our perceptions, we do not thereby invalidate our knowledge of God and at the same time trust the rest of our knowledge. Nevertheless, as Robert B. McLeod again says, the psychologists have taught us that "the self is to be considered as one significant structure in a total psychological field" and that our perception of reality is directly affected by the "stability or instability of the self." [18] In other words, no psychology of knowing is complete without a psychology of the self.

Yet there is a point at which the reality-character of the world and of God operates quite independently of our wishes, our hopes, our stabilities, and our instabilities. Reality, in and of itself, has a toughness of its own that is not touched by the distortions or personal propensities of our self-concepts, dreams, or aspirations. A square is not a circle, a table is not a chair, a door is not a solid wall, the Bible is not a dictionary, the church was not established yesterday, and Jesus of Nazareth was not Buddha! Furthermore, when someone begins to protest too much and to say that all these things are products of our wishes, having been shaped by our own need for protection, then we are forced to conclude that he, too, has need for protection. He, too, is filled with the hope that an exact scientific statement of reality in its totality is entirely and immediately possible. He, too, is filled with the hope that man *can* have a *perfectly intelligible* and reasonable relation with regard to his fellow man and to nature. These in themselves are wishes and hopes. They are illusions, subject to the same test of reality which their authors apply to religion. Thus we hit one of the solid limitations of the psychologist's task. He can help us to measure the processes underneath our experience of God. He can give us empirical descriptions of the more proximate and mediate reality of the world. As a philosopher and as a religious person he can join with us in our search after the nature of ultimate reality and in our quest for God. Or he can refuse to join with us for his own personal reasons. Whatever he concludes, his beliefs and his philosophical presuppositions are subject to the same laws as ours. His great contribution to us, however, is to help us understand more precisely the distortions, the "baffling reflections" and the confusions created by the instability of the self as we seek to perceive God. A much more positive contribution would be to bring us accurate, dependable descriptions of the stable, mature, productive adult's experience of religion. What is it that makes the ordinary person who seems to be religious a productive and creative person, if indeed he is?

Increasingly, psychologists today are saying with Gordon Allport that "the healthy person in possession of normal intelligence, insight, and emotional maturity knows that he cannot solve life's problems by wishful thinking or cure his own partialness by fictionizing." He says that "the developed person will not fabricate his religion out of some emotional fragment but will seek a theory of Being in which all fragments are meaningfully ordered." In other words, he will have a *comprehensive* religious sentiment and even then will realize the finiteness, incompleteness, and partialness of his understanding to such an extent that his religious world view will produce in him humility rather than arrogance.[14] The psychologists of personality help us most at this point. In Allport's words, "As a science psychology can neither prove nor disprove religion's claims to truth. It can, however, help explain why these claims are so many and so diverse. . . . The final truths of religion are unknown, but a psychology that impedes understanding of the religious potentialities of man scarcely deserves to be called a logos of the human psyche at all." [15]

Whereas psychology has pointed out how religion can be a retreat from reality, psychology also in many instances has emphasized the role of religious concern in the "striving for" reality. Allport calls attention to Kurt Goldstein's doctrine of self-actualization as an example of this. Likewise, he mentions the more recent psychoanalytic conception of the "fortified ego" which is able to resist the temptations of impulse and distractions of environment and to persist in productive and creative work and the pursuit of contemplative ideals. This leads to the unification of personality and a transcending of conflict.

Andres Angyal, another psychologist of personality, speaks of the "setting" of the personality. He says that there are various "sets" of attitudes either which are subordinated to or which take precedence over each other in the total organization of personality. Angyal describes the way in which a given "set" of personality may determine the total direction of the person's existence and form his whole system of axioms for behavior. The pointing of the direction of this "main meaning" of the life is either toward or away from reality, but not necessarily either. Robert McLeod says, as a psychologist, that what impresses him about the genuinely religious man is "his serenity, his courage, his loyalty, the firmness of his faith, his conviction that life has a deep meaning and that whatever happens to him as an individual is relatively unimportant compared with that which is greater than himself.[16]

Psychology has done much to help us to produce this kind of person in that it has made us intensely aware of the distortions, disharmonies, and retreats from reality which prevent and even caricature the virtues of which McLeod has spoken. Psychology has spoken. Psychology has spoken to us much of reality, but one of the main points at which psychology has been silent is in helping us to define what reality is. At this point psychologists are vaguer and more nebulous and less specific than either the philosophers, the theologians, or the other scientists. Nevertheless, if they were to attempt to define reality and give us clear leadership at this point, they would have to draw upon their earlier parentage in philosophy and theology for information, techniques, insights, and wisdom, for this is essentially a philosophical and theological task.

The Christian theologians have through the centuries grappled with the slippery difference between illusion and reality. They have, since the apostle Paul, been more or less aware of the imperfection of their grasp of Ultimate Love. They have known, to varying degrees of conviction, that their vision of God has been but "baffling reflections" seen "darkly" in a mirror. The point of departure for them has always been in their confrontation of the Person of the Lord Jesus Christ. Revelation before him was in a different manner and piecemeal. In him God, as he is in himself, and man in his perfected essence were made one. The necessity felt by Feuerbach to identify God as the perfected man and the skepticism of Freud as to the validity of man's knowledge of the Ultimate in God meet in resolution in the Person of Christ, the God-man. Surjit Singh, a converted Sikh and professor of philosophy at San Francisco Theological Seminary, states that we as Christians "start neither from man nor from God. These two starting points are not at our disposal." We do not start either with God, as such, nor with man, as such. Both of these are abstractions. We build our understanding of the self of man and the person of God on the revelation we have seen historically in Jesus Christ. In him, "the Word was made flesh, and dwelt among us (and we beheld his glory . . .) full of grace and truth." [17] He *is* reality.

The question confronted by Christian theologians, even if they are phrased in different words and philosophical frames of orientation, will nevertheless be the questions the psychologist will face as he tries to give his followers a clear understanding of what he means by "reality." The Christian theologian, as he joins in the search with the psychologist, will find the broad outlines of theology being given more specific and detailed analysis and synthesis in the data which have been discovered by psychologists in their research into the nature of man.

The psychologist should not be excluded from the task of theology and philosophy. More than that, he should be invited into the conversation, for the fact remains, he cannot be exempt from it. But as he enters the inquiry room, he, too, will have to check his dogmas at the door just as he has insisted that the philosopher and the theologian do! He has admitted that man cannot live without a main meaning to his life, and he has joined efforts with those who seek to formulate clear guidance for mankind and with mankind as to the ultimate nature of reality, the main purpose for living, and the enduring reasons for being. Many psychologists have joined in this conversation and quest. They have accented the necessity for meaning in life. They have emphasized the importance of the durability of man's ultimate loyalties in life. We turn to them now in order to hear what they have to say about religion.

Chapter 7

RELIGION: THE SEARCH FOR ULTIMATE MEANING IN LIFE

As we look back over what psychology has said thus far about religion, we see four stages in this conversation. First, we see psychology as a silent science when it comes to having anything to say about religion. For instance, I. P. Pavlov (1849-1936) worked patiently and diligently at devising experiments through which he could validate such a concept as the conditioned reflex. In 1904 he was awarded the Nobel prize in physiology and medicine for work on digestive glands. Walter B. Cannon (1871-1945) developed controlled devices for studying the bodily changes associated with pain, fear, and hunger. He laid much of the groundwork for the psychosomatic concept of medicine, which emphasizes the psychological component in illness. He gave us an awesome discussion of the intricate "wisdom of the body." But these men are not known for proclamations about religion; only a few psychologists spoke as noisily about religion as did John B. Watson.

In the second phase of what psychology has to say about religion, we find a blatant, noisy rejection. This characterizes some of the more extreme statements of persons like Watson and Sigmund Freud. In their feverish attempts to make a religion of psychology itself, they pronounced all religious predecessors as either fools or children. At the same time they overlooked the fact that their objections and ideas were subject to the same criticism themselves. Yet their successors have been quick to modify these criticisms, even though they retain fidelity to the solid empirical research unearthed by their teachers. The psychoanalytic movement itself has been split asunder several times by the inability of its leaders to "stand for" disagreement with their ideas.

In the third phase we find psychologists with a critical but cautiously affectionate attitude toward religion. This characterizes the keen distinctions and challenging valuations of men like Adolph Meyer, Gordon Allport, Erich Fromm, and Karl Menninger. These men approach religion with mingled emotions. They give us the benefit both of their basic criticisms and their profound, positive conviction. They have helped to clarify, purify, and redirect some of our more hidden motives for being religious. As John Baillie, an eminent theologian, has said, they have helped us to be more specific in our confession of sin. They have helped us to a wiser humility and a more single-hearted loyalty to that which we perceive as the Ultimate Claim upon our lives.

The fourth phase of contemporary psychology's contributions to the discussion of religion is the most recent one. Since 1950 several psychologists have begun to speak with an unhampered voice of conviction on the subject of religion. They speak with an authenticity both as persons in their own right as well as representatives of their profession. These psychologists have discovered the living, beating pulse of spirituality as it is psychologically perceived. Religion at its best in the healthy adult, to these psychologists, consists of the ultimate meanings by which a person lives and for which he has chosen both to live and, if necessary, to die.

In the re-evaluation of the psychology of meaningfulness in life and of the psychology of loyalty, these psychologists are picking up the trail of the thought of Josiah Royce (1855-1916). The idealism of Royce was centered in what he called "the philosophy of loyalty." He defined loyalty as "*the will to manifest, so far as possible, the Eternal, that is, the conscious and super-human unity of life, in the form of acts of an individual Self.*" He further insisted that loyalty "*is the will to believe in something eternal and to express that belief in the practical life of a human being.*" [1] In other words, the integration of personality rests largely upon the integrity, durability, and eternal nature of the object of loyalty around which personality is integrated. When the central meaning, the main object of loyalty, is never discovered, or proves to be false, perishes by death, or for any reason collapses, the person must either discover a new center, a new loyalty, or perish himself of sheer meaninglessness.

Religion and the threat of meaninglessness. Psychologists today in increasingly larger numbers are calling attention to the way in which the lives of adults are being drained of meaning, filled with boredom, and fraught with anxiety as a result. Carl G. Jung draws a distinction between those patients who are suffering from a "clinically definable neurosis" and those who are overwhelmed by "having their lives on their hands," having nothing to do with their lives, and suffering from the sheer meaninglessness and purposelessness of their being. Jung, therefore, in his system of psychology has sought to tackle the problem at a deeper level. He saw Freud's penetrating criticism of religion which amounted to outright rejection. He, therefore, was far more cautious and discriminating in his evaluation of religion, and used "his whole scientific equipment to bring to light its significance for man's psychic life." [2] Jung says that when a person feels called into loyalty to a given object, he does so with meaningfulness and comprehensiveness. "When a problem is taken religiously," he says it means, psychologically speaking, that "it is taken as something very significant, of particular value, as something that affects the whole of a man and therefore also the unconscious." [3] Then these attitudes become absolute, for "any absolute attitude is always a religious attitude." He further says that "at whatever point a man becomes absolute, then you will find his religion." [4]

The absolutes by which men live are not merely opinions they halfheartedly hold. They are meanings and values for which they live and are willing to die. Gotthard Booth, a psychoanalyst, says that he has "theoretical and empirical reasons" for believing that the health of either a devout Christian or of a militant atheist is better than that of the person who has "found nothing in the world for which he wants to live and die." [5]

In short, both Jung and Booth are saying that a person's basic beliefs are matters of life and death to him. He suffers as a total person when his life is not endowed with the vocation, the calling, the meaning, the ultimate *raison d'être*. Religion at its heart, to a given person, is that master motive of his being, that essential meaning of his existence.

The fact remains that the depth and extent of the meaninglessness of individual and corporate life today poses one of the poignant threats of our existence. The despair of modern man is written in his hopelessness. We can say with Bernard Shaw: "What is hope? A form of moral responsibility. Here [in hell] there is no hope, and consequently no duty, no work, nothing to be gained by praying, nothing to be lost by doing what you like. Hell, in short, is a place where you have nothing to do but amuse yourself." [6] This is the antithesis of the meaningful spiritual life, for, to quote Paul Tillich, "The anxiety of meaninglessness is anxiety about the loss of an ultimate concern, of a meaning which gives meaning to all meanings. This anxiety is aroused by a loss of the spiritual center, of an answer, however symbolic and indirect, to the question to the meaning of existence." [7] When this happens one is compelled to flit from one object of devotion to another, "because the meaning of each of them vanishes and . . . is transformed into indifference or aversion. Everything is tried and nothing satisfies." [8] The meaninglessness of our age is epitomized in a poem by Minou Drouet, an eight-year-old French girl, when she describes her heart as an "empty boat" whose harbor is "Nowhere." [9]

To this emptiness and meaninglessness, psychology, during its earlier stage of negative generalizations about religion, tended to contribute. As Robert B. McLeod states it, "in contemporary psychology, religion tends to be something secondary to be reduced, something peculiar to be explained away, or something of practical value to be exploited." [10] However, from such standpoints of education—explaining away and exploitation—psychologists have moved to a much more serious search for the essential meaning of life. Psychology, says Lawrence Cole, has had to face up to the basic values which it will espouse. The messianic hope of science as *the* ultimate meaning of life has been radically shaken by the events of the years since Freud set forth this particular illusion. Now psychologists are in a stage of reconstruction.

Even earlier, a voice bearing clear, positive contributions to a meaningful psychological interpretation of life was effectively opposed by Freud. It was the voice of Alfred Adler (1870-1937). He emphasized the need for co-operative endeavor between the religious and psychological interpretation of man. He said that the materialistic kind of psychology "lacks the goal, which after all is the essence of life," but that "the religious view," far ahead in the provision of goals for life, "lacks the causal foundation, for God cannot be proven scientifically; He is the gift of faith. . . . God as man's goal is the harmonic complementation for the groping and erring movements in the path of life. . . . It certainly was a non-verbal, non-conceptual insight of religious fervor in which the sacred writing of man with the goal setting God first took place, as it still takes place today in the religious soul." [11] This Adler says under the discussion of "the sanctification of human relations."

Psychologists, particularly since World War II, have discovered that if you can show man a piece of what he as a religious person would call God's work to do (and which he has more recently learned to call by new names) you can make him entirely reckless of the consequences to himself personally. You have endowed him with courage for his existence, what Paul Tillich has called "the courage to be."

One of these psychologists is Viktor Frankl, a Viennese psychiatrist, who was captured and held in a concentration camp in Germany during World War II. He points out that whereas the neurotic inclines to play one task off against another and to avoid basic responsibility, "an essential characteristic of the religious man is that he is a man who is conscious of and responsible toward . . . his life mission." He experiences his "task" as coming from an authority . . . and experiences "the task as a mission, a mandate." Therefore Frankl has devised what he calls "existential analysis" which aims at "bringing the patient to the point of the highest possible concentration and dedication." He says that "it is our business, then, to show how the life of every man has a unique goal to which only one single course leads. . . . If the patient should object that he does not know the meaning of his life, the unique potentialities of his existence are not apparent to him, then we can only reply that his primary task is just this: to find his way to his own proper task; to advance toward the uniqueness and singularity of his own meaning in life." [12] Concerning religion, as such, Frankl says: "From the psychological point of view, the religious person is one who experiences not only what is spoken, but the speaker as well; that is, his hearing is sharper than the non-religious person. In the dialogue with his conscience—in this most intimate of possible monologues—his God is his interlocutor. . . . For a person religious in this sense the experiencing of God means the experiencing the ultimate 'Other Self.' "[13]

The character of this Other Self of whom Frankl speaks is referred to only negatively by modern psychology. Psychologically relevant theologians such as Martin Buber and Reinhold Niebuhr see the self in dialogue with itself and with God in a personal encounter. The psychological gist of this relationship can be evaluated as a phenomenon. However, the character of the values, goals, purposes, intentions, and for that matter the self itself are facts. We need both a careful psychological methodology and psychologists who themselves are mature enough to look at these facts with an unbiased eye and to let those facts speak for themselves. But we know enough at this point from what the psychologists say to trace a brief biography of the psychologists' attitude toward religion as such. In the beginning, psychologists took the ancient Greek maxim which said: "Know thyself." As the psychology of personality and, particularly, psychoanalytic studies of the self grew, psychologists took the maxim of the age of enlightenment: "Be thyself." As psychologists have come through the shaking of the foundations of our culture and of our civilization more recently, they are considering more seriously the maxim of the Christian faith, which does not exclude the other two maxims, but puts them in their right perspective, namely, "Give thyself."

Only recently has the question of suffering and self-sacrifice been seriously considered in a positive light by contemporary psychology. Usually this has been "reduced to" a "martyr-complex" or written off as self-punishment. But Viktor Frankl challenges the tacit hedonism of much psychological theory by saying that "for the inner biography of man, grief and repentance," suffering and self-giving do have meaning. Human life, he says, "*can be fulfilled not only in creating and enjoying, but also in suffering*." [14] Suffering may mature, season, and endow the life with new meaning. In saying this he cuts at the nerve of interpretation of religion as "success." He says that "*lack of success does not signify the lack of meaning*." Truly great religion has grown out of great suffering in which the self has been elevated to an overview of the suffering which enabled him to grasp its ultimate as well as its immediate meaning. Such was the experience of the apostle Paul when he said: "Blessed be God, even the Father of our Lord Jesus Christ, the Father of mercies, and the God of all comfort; who comforteth us in all our tribulation, that we may be able to comfort them which are in any trouble, by the comfort wherewith we ourselves are comforted of God." [15] But when we ask what is worth suffering for, it becomes necessary for us to think of the psychology of the future. We must go beyond psychology as it now stands if we are to have any clear understanding of that to which or to whom man is to give himself.

Chapter 8

THE PSYCHOLOGY "BEYOND PSYCHOLOGY"

Gardner Murphy, of the Menninger Clinic and psychology editor for Harper & Brothers, in one of the concluding sections of his monumental work on personality, says that "there may be a touch of neurotic phobia" in the way in which the psychological study of man "has evaded the question" of man's "need in some way to come to terms with the cosmos as a whole." He says that in a future psychology of personality psychologists must directly grapple with the question "of man's response to the cosmos, his sense of unity with it, the nature of his aesthetic demands upon it, and his feelings of loneliness or of consummation in his contemplation of it." He feels that the methodology of the future must "pulverize" the knowledge of personality which we have at present and that no "inexcusable dogmatism" on the part of psychologists can prevent them from facing up to a study of man's responses "to the cosmos to which he is a reflection."[1]

In another place in the same book, Gardner Murphy tells the story of how before the intrepid sailors of the fifteenth century discovered the Western Hemisphere, the coins of Portugal bore the inscription of *Ne Plus Ultra.* Above this inscription was a picture of the Pillars of Hercules. After the discovery of the West, the coins carried the same picture, but the Latin word *ne* was removed from the inscription beneath. This changed the whole meaning of the phrase from "There is nothing beyond" to "There is more beyond."

Psychologists have stood at the gates of sensory experience and said that there is nothing beyond the perceptions and wishes of men. They have stood at the gates of the known methodology and said that a realm of experience was *not* unless it could be studied by their methods. However, a few of them have sailed the uncharted regions with the philosophers and theologians. They have come back saying: "There is more beyond." What do they say about the character of this "beyondness"?

A less well-known psychoanalyst, Otto Rank,

just before his death in 1939, wrote his first book in English. He had come to this country as a refugee from Europe. The Foreword of his book says that "while it contains the essence of Rank's old world scholarship, [it] reveals the *beyond* of a new life that he found for himself in this country." Rank himself says that in this book he has attempted to "picture human life" not merely as he studied it for more than a generation, but as he had achieved it for himself in experience, "beyond the compulsion to change it in accordance with any man-made ideology." Interestingly enough he entitled the book, *Beyond Psychology*. He pointed to a crisis in psychology as it stands today, underlining the fact that psychological theory is shaped by the spiritual ideology most prevalent in its day, even as any other theory is also shaped. Therefore, he began to reach gropingly for that larger frame of reference in which man not only talks and thinks but in which he lives existentially. He began to try to discern the "beyondness of psychology." He has given us some real help in marking out this uncharted region of the future of psychology.

We are tempted, when we try to get beyond

psychology, to fall into the assumption that we have done so by turning to a social or collective psychology. We do this by shifting from a purely individual psychology which conceives the individual as an isolated entity within himself to an interpersonal psychology which emphasizes the relationships that go on *between* people. However, even here we have not developed an adequate understanding of the uncharted realms of human nature. This can restrict the spiritual life to the noisy demands of society, and his religion will be merely the sum total of his social relationships, raised to the nth degree. Rank said that he himself had to go beyond this. He concluded that there is a basis of human nature—which must be reached—which lies "beyond any psychology, individual or collective." He declares that "modern psychology has attempted the impossible." It has sought " to rationalize the rational." He says that there is something about the human being which "does not fit into our rational schemes of things." Therefore, "it is not sufficient to *see* the importance of the irrational element in human life and point it out in *rational* terms!" The more we do this the more we see that "man is born beyond psychology and he dies beyond it, but he can *live* beyond it only through vital experience of his own–in religious terms, through revelation, conversion or rebirth." Even philosophical and theological rationalizations of this happening are inadequate, and we must go beyond them. As Alfred Adler expressed it, these insights are nonverbal, nonconceptual. We must go beyond these verbalisms, not as some hero, artist, or a neurotic appears upon the stage of life only to go down unmasked, undressed, and unpretentious, but to arise as "human beings who require no interpreter." [2]

Psychologists today have become more and more concerned about this "rebirth" of the self of which Rank speaks. As they thrust themselves upon research for an adequate religious world view, their conversations have said three things. First, they have sought to disentangle religious experience from its cultural and institutional forms of expression. They have distinguished between "religion" and "religious experience." John Dewey, for instance, says that the supernatural dogmas of religion have weakened and sapped man's religious attitude, and that "the opposition between religious values as I can see them and religions is not to be bridged. Just because the release of these values is so important, that identification with the creeds and cults of religions must be dissolved."[3] Working through the processes of secular education, psychologists of education have defined this "common faith" of Dewey in terms of "moral and spiritual values." They have systematically reduced religious experience to the least common denominator of all the great religious heritages of mankind. Likewise, C. G. Jung sharply demarcated "religion" from worship and dogma, "discerning that the effect of the Church was to obstruct the growth of any real and personal religion. . . ."[4] An unintended side-effect of the effort to transcend the cultural idiosyncrasies of religion, however, is to disembody religious values and experience from vital relationship to the churches. Religious experience may become so etherealized that the institutional structure of the churches is neglected. More often this neglect leaves the churches to the more primitive and unreflective elements of the community, thereby perpetuating the very thing the psychologist is seeking to offset. This is the social unrealism, however of much sophisticated thinking about religion, and is not particularly characteristic of psychologists. Quite often it is true of theological professors!

A second approach apparent in the thought and activity of psychologists as they go "beyond" empirical psychology into the realm of religion itself emerges in their fascination with interpretations of life and the world which tend to depersonalize the ultimate nature and destiny of man and God. One example of this is found in Gardner Murphy's monumental work on personality. He speaks of the "fundamental unity of which individual personalities are droplets." [5] When he speaks of psychologists of personality integrating their findings "with older insights of an intuitive or poetic sort," we wonder to what kind of resources he is referring. We rather get the feeling that he is referring to some sort of pantheism, and not to the distinctly personal theism of the Christian faith. The "fundamental unity of which individual personalities are droplets" could easily be given a Buddhist slant, because to the Buddhist the final goal of the religious man is to escape into blissful nonexistence from existence. This is called *nirvana*, which is a Sanskrit word originally meaning annihilation. Whether Murphy is talking out of this background or not is difficult to say, because his writings do not specifically discuss this issue. Nevertheless, the depersonalization evident here runs counter to a distinctly personal destiny for man and character of God.

This accents the imperative need for an avowedly Christian interpretation of the data of psychologists as to the nature and goals of personality. A few psychologists, in the third place, have become articulate at this point. This does not mean that they have begun to bend the facts discovered by psychologists to fit the Christian conception of personality. Rather, this means that these psychologists are personally and professionally secure enough to take the Christian conception of man and evaluate it without a wholesale feeling of rejection or an idolatrous need to become a dogmatist.

In something of this balanced perspective Otto Rank speaks quite clearly. Rank, in a chapter entitled "The Creation of Personality," says that "the Christian religion cannot be disposed of as a mere development of Hellenistic ideas of redemption but is an original religion of its own to which only the religious systems of the Far East are comparable in spirituality."[6] Rank thoroughly discusses the apostle Paul's interpretation of his conversion at Damascus as the bringing back of the Lord Jesus Christ from the dead in Paul's very self, whereby he himself, Paul, was "risen from the dead, alive, no longer waiting for an indefinite future to live the life on earth." He points out that this resurrection of Christ in man is "available as a personal experience to everybody in the present" and "the average man" may thereby acquire "a new self" and become "prototype for the average man, in fact, for mankind."

Rank says that the Christian understanding of the creation of a new personality, a new self, discards the Oriental conception of rebirth as well as the after-life conception of the Jews in terms of the resurrection of the body. In its place is a new kind of being in the here and now, a creation of a new personality, the birth of a new life in Christ.[7] This is not a redemption for privileged individuals or groups but a spiritualized conception of the birth of a new life for every individual, for all mankind. Rank says that the apostle Paul set forth an understanding of the dynamic therapy of human life which "created Selfhood." In referring to the death of Jesus Christ, he says that "this is no sacrifice or atonement for a rebellion against God the Father, but an expression of the liberated individual who feels master of his own life and death and free to choose a Father if he wants to." [8] Furthermore he says that Christianity, "as far as we know, represents the only successful attempt to form a reconciling principle in the reciprocated love of God to man." [9] Rank, expressing the hope for a revival of the Christian philosophy of life to counteract the anti-ideologies of modern secular religion, says that "the masses are still deeply engulfed in religious traditions of their forefathers, and the mere fact that a handful of intellectuals have introduced a few new terms into popular language does not alter the deep religious feeling most people, including those intellectuals themselves, cherish in spite of their denial." [10]

These affirmations of Otto Rank are relatively unique in the literature of contemporary psychology. However, they do represent the efforts of one psychologist to get into the "beyond situation" to which the basic data of the field of psychology, especially the psychology of personality, inevitably tend to lead the psychologists.

Nevertheless, these contributions of Rank are more to be classed in the realm of personal reflection than in the discharge of his role as a research man in psychology. The main need of religion in relation to psychology is for a more specifically adapted scientific method for studying the religious life and behavior of people. Talcott Parsons is right when he says that Christianity is *one* of the parents of science. We have moved on the assumption that science is one source of the revelation of God, that is, that he can become known through his works. Parsons says that "it is not by chance that Christian civilization has been the mother of science . . . the scientific study of religion itself is a development which is a logical and inevitable outcome of Christianity itself." [11]

But a given branch of science has to develop a marked degree of maturity in order to be even partly objective about its "mother," Christianity. We began by saying that psychology is a *young* science, that it is in the process of maturity. Otto Rank called it the "last and youngest child of religion." [12] Maybe we are expecting too much to ask now that the *youngest* child of our faith be most objective about its mother. But ask it, nevertheless we shall.

We are demanding a maturity of psychology that it has only recently begun to promise, much less produce. We are asking for a psychology that tackles big problems and seeks methods whereby they may be solved rather than tackling small problems because they happen to fit the methods of study the psychologist already knows about. In Robert McLeod's words, "the techniques of traditional psychology have so far failed to give us a good psychology of religion. If we are to design new and more adequate techniques, we must begin by attempting to suspend our traditional heroes and take a fresh look at the phenomena." [13] We need a psychology whose function is to raise questions that need to be asked because of their importance and not because some neat method has already been devised.

Yet, this is to lay a burden of responsibility also upon the Christian theologian as well. Emil Brunner, the renowned Swiss theologian, has said, "There *is* a psychology which, at least in part, is not affected by either faith or unbelief, a knowledge of facts about man which the Christian must weave into his picture of man like anyone else." [14] Also "Karl Barth has said that this knowledge, as such, cannot be an enemy of the Christian confession of faith." [15]

This body of knowledge must be mastered by theologians just as the content of the Christian faith must become a part of the psychologist's education, if a distinctly Christian understanding of the psychology of religion is to emerge. The final questions of psychology are the beginning concerns of religion. We can give thanks for the patient endeavors of contemporary psychologists who have worked in the boundary situations between a purely mechanical interpretation of life and the distinctly purposive interpretations which characterize the Christian faith. They have brought us up to the Promised Land of the

Christian faith and reminded us that just as God is our Creator and we are his creatures, just as he is in Christ our Redeemer and we are the object of his Love in Christ, even so creation continues in the miracle of human personality.

A LAYMAN'S READING COURSE IN PSYCHOLOGY AND RELIGION

The following books are suggested as a cumulative series of books for the layman to read. They should be read in the order in which they are listed. They move from the simple to the more complex. The aim is to help the lay person, on his own, to develop a "background" in psychology as it is related to religion.

1. Gardner Murphy, *An Introduction to Psychology* (New York: Harper & Brothers, 1951, 583 pages). This is an introductory textbook. It is a unified and systematic approach to the fundamentals of psychology, utilizing a viewpoint developed primarily in the study of personality.

2. Robert S. Woodworth, *Contemporary Schools of Psychology*, Revised Edition (New York: The Ronald Press Company, 1951). This book takes up each of the different schools of psychology, such as structuralism, Gestalt psychology, psychoanalysis, and traces its history, leading personalities, main teachings, and present status.

3. William James, *Varieties of Religious Experience* (New York: Modern Library, 1902). An old but still influential classic by one of the greatest psychologists of all time.

4. Gordon W. Allport, *The Individual and His Religion* (New York: The Macmillan Company, 1950). The meaning of religion in the personal life

is studied carefully by a psychologist who is a practicing Christian. This book is particularly helpful for the college student who is studying psychology for the first time.

5. Gordon W. Allport, *Becoming: Basic Considerations for a Psychology of Personality* (New Haven: Yale University Press, 1955). The Terry Lectures at Yale, presented in careful and polished form, giving definite references to the religious sentiment of mankind.

6. Paul E. Johnson, *The Psychology of Religion* (Nashville, Tenn.: Abingdon Press, 1945). A clearly written survey of the ways in which psychology has been applied to religion since about 1850.

7. Erich Fromm, *Psychoanalysis and Religion* (New Haven: Yale University Press, 1950). A contemporary psychoanalyst describes the various positions of psychoanalysis about religion and sets forth his own interpretation.

8. C. G. Jung, *Psychology and Religion* (New Haven: Yale University Press, 1938). A definitive statement by Jung which should be read only after having read Jolan Jacobi's small book, *The Psychology of Jung* (New Haven: Yale University Press, 1943). This latter book gives a brief, simply written and authorized statement of Jung's psychological system.

9. Lewis J. Sherrill, *The Struggle of the Soul*, (New York: The Macmillan Company, 1951). This is a synthesized use of "the best of modern psychology" in an interpretation of the religious growth of a person.

10. Wayne E. Oates, *Religious Factors in Mental*

Illness (New York: Association Press, 1955). A detailed evaluation of the ways in which religion may help or hinder the understanding, treatment, and recovery of a mentally ill person.

11. Wayne E. Oates, *Religious Dimensions of Personality* (New York: Association Press, 1957). A systematic study of the psychology of religion using the Christian understanding of personality as a central organizing principle.

12. Paul Tillich, *The Courage to Be* (New Haven: Yale University Press, 1952). A theologian gives his analysis of the anxiety of our times, using contemporary psychology as background material.

13. David Roberts, *Psychotherapy and a Christian View of Man* (New York: Charles Scribner's Sons, 1951). A Christian theologian who himself was psychoanalyzed describes the deeper appreciation of his theological heritage which resulted from his psychotherapy.

14. Albert Outler, *Psychotherapy and the Christian Message* (New York: Charles Scribner's Sons, 1954). Another theologian draws the philosophical and theological issues between psychotherapy and Christian theology into clear focus and gives his own dependable answer.

NOTES BY CHAPTERS

Chapter 1. *What Is Psychology?*

1. Carl R. Rogers, "A Personal Formulation of Client-Centered Therapy," *Marriage and Family Living*, Vol. XIV, No. 4, Nov., 1952, p. 342.
2. Kurt Lewin, *Principles of Topological Psychology* (New York: McGraw-Hill Book Company, 1936), p. 5.
3. Harry Stack Sullivan, *The Interpersonal Theory of Psychiatry* (New York: W. W. Norton & Company, Inc., 1952), pp. 19-25.
4. New York: The Macmillan Company, rev. ed. 1955. Or Modern Library edition, No. 96.

Chapter 2. *Where Psychology Is Silent About Religion*

1. Paul Tillich, "Communicating the Gospel," *Union Seminary Quarterly Review*, Vol. VII, June, 1952, No. 4, p. 3.
2. Ernest Jones, *The Life and Work of Sigmund Freud* (New York: Basic Books, Inc., 1953), Vol. I, pp. 19, 22-23.
3. Robert B. McLeod, *Religious Perspectives in the Teaching of Experimental Psychology* (New Haven, Conn.: The Hazen Foundation, 1950), p. 6.

CHAPTER 3. *Religion: Bondage to Idols or Freedom for Growth?*

1. Liston Pope, *Millhands and Preachers* (New Haven: Yale University Press, 1942), p. 332.
2. Talcott Parsons, *Religious Perspectives of College Teaching in Sociology and Social Psychology* (New Haven, Conn.: The Hazen Foundation, 1951), pp. 24-25.
3. Sigmund Freud, "Civilized Sexual Morality and Modern Nervousness," *Collected Papers* (London: Hogarth Press, 1949), Vol. II, pp. 76-99.
4. Parsons, *op. cit.*, p. 37.
5. Isaiah 2:8.
6. Galatians 5:1. (RSV)
7. O. T. Binkley, *The Churches and the Social Conscience* (Indianapolis: National Foundation Press, 1948), p. 4.
8. Erich Fromm, *Escape from Freedom* (New York: Farrar and Rinehart, 1941), pp. 31-37.
9. *Ibid.*, p. 38.
10. *Ibid.*, pp. 104, 140-141.
11. Anton Boisen, "Freud, Jung, and Fromm," *Pastoral Psychology*, Oct., 1951, p. 52.
12. *Saturday Review of Literature*, Feb. 10, 1951, pp. 34, 39.
13. *Annals of the American Academy of Sciences*, Jan., 1951.
14. Matthew 23:9.
15. Rollo May, *The Meaning of Anxiety* (New York: The Ronald Press Company, 1950), p. 110.

16. T. W. Adorno and Associates, *The Authoritarian Personality* (New York: Harper & Brothers, 1950).
17. Erich Fromm, *Psychoanalysis and Religion* (New Haven: Yale University Press, 1950), pp. 35-37, 117.

CHAPTER 4. *Religion: Childishness or a Way to Maturity?*

1. Princeton, N. J.: Princeton University Press, 1941.
2. Horace Bushnell, "The Kingdom of Heaven as a Grain of Mustard Seed," *The New Englander*, Vol. II, Oct., 1844, pp. 600-619.
3. Sigmund Freud, *The Future of an Illusion*, tr. by W. D. Robson Scott (New York: Liveright Publishing Corporation, 1949), pp. 41-42.
4. *Ibid.*, p. 82.
5. J. C. Flügel, *Men, Morals, and Society* (New York: International Universities Press, Inc., 1945), pp. 272-273.
6. Gordon W. Allport, *Becoming: Basic Considerations for Psychology and Personality* (New Haven: Yale University Press, 1955), pp. 94, 95.
7. *Ibid.*
8. Gordon W. Allport, *The Individual and His Religion* (New York: The Macmillan Company, 1950), p. 142.
9. Harry Stack Sullivan, *The Interpersonal Theory of Psychiatry* (New York: W. W. Norton & Company, Inc., 1953), p. 34.

10. Gordon W. Allport, *op. cit.* in note 8, pp. 67-69.
11. Leon J. Saul, *Emotional Maturity* (Philadelphia: J. B. Lippincott Company, 1947), p. 107.
12. Hebrews 5: 12-14.

CHAPTER 5. *Religion: A Sickness or a Way to Health?*

1. New York: Association Press, 1955.
2. Erich Fromm, *Psychoanalysis and Religion* (New Haven: Yale University Press, 1950), p. 6.
3. *Collected Papers* (London: Hogarth Press, 1949), Vol. II, pp. 25-35.
4. Sigmund Freud, *The Future of an Illusion* (London: Hogarth Press, 1949), pp. 76-77.
5. Sigmund Freud, *Civilization and Its Discontents* (London: Hogarth Press, 1946), p. 23.
6. Paul Bergman, "A Religious Conversion in the Course of Psychotherapy," *American Journal of Psychotherapy*, Vol. 7, No. 1, Jan., 1953, pp. 41-58.
7. Harry M. Tiebout, "Conversion as a Psychological Phenomenon in the Treatment of the Alcoholic," *The American Journal of Psychiatry*, Jan., 1944.
8. Leon Salzman, "The Psychology of Religious Ideological Conversion," *Psychiatry*, Vol. XVI, No. 2, May, 1953.
9. Alphonse Maeder, *Ways to Psychic Health* (New York: Charles Scribner's Sons, 1953), p. 11.

10. Alphonse Maeder, *op. cit.*, p. 176.
11. Erich Fromm, *op. cit.*, p. 117.
12. Erich Fromm, *Psychoanalysis and Religion* (New Haven: Yale University Press, 1950), p. 118.

CHAPTER 6. *Religion: An Illusion or a Way to Reality?*

1. *Religious Perspectives of College Teaching in Experimental Psychology* (New Haven, Conn.: The Hazen Foundation, 1950), p. 14.
2. Ludwig Feuerbach, *Das Wesen des Christentums*, p. 282. Quoted by Karl Barth in "An Introductory Essay" to Feuerbach's *The Essence of Christianity* (New York: Harper & Brothers, 1957), p. xix.
3. *The Essence of Christianity*, *op. cit.* p. 15.
4. Barth in Feuerbach's *The Essence of Christianity*, op. cit., p. xv.
5. Feuerbach, *op. cit.*, p. 14.
6. *Ibid.*, pp. 16-17.
7. *Ibid.*, p. 143.
8. Karl Marx, *Capital: A Critique of Political Economy*, tr. by Moore and Aveling (Chicago: Charles H. Kerr and Co., 1921), Vol. I, pp. 91-92.
9. Sigmund Freud, *The Future of an Illusion*, tr. by W. D. Robson Scott (New York: Liveright Publishing Corporation, 1949), p. 52.
10. Sigmund Freud, *Civilization and Its Discontents* (London: Hogarth Press, 1946), p. 24.
11. *Ibid.*, p. 42.

12. Hebrews 11:1.
13. Robert B. McLeod, *Religious Perspectives in the Teaching of Experimental Psychology* (New Haven, Conn.: The Hazen Foundation, 1950), p. 16.
14. Gordon W. Allport, *Becoming: Basic Considerations for a Psychology of Personality* (New Haven: Yale University Press, 1955), p. 96.
15. *Ibid.*
16. Robert B. McLeod, *Religious Perspectives in the Teaching of Experimental Psychology* (New Haven, Conn.: The Hazen Foundation, 1950), p. 13.
17. John 1:14.

CHAPTER 7. *Religion: The Search for Ultimate Meaning in Life*

1. Josiah Royce, *The Philosophy of Loyalty* (New York: The Macmillan Company, 1908), p. 357.
2. Hans Schaer, *Religion and the Cure of Souls in Jung's Psychology* (New York: Pantheon Books, Inc., 1950), p. 15.
3. C. G. Jung, *Psychological Types*, tr. by H. G. Baynes (New York: Harcourt, Brace & Company, Inc., 1938), p. 274.
4. C. G. Jung, *Seelenprobleme der Gegenwart*, p. 107, quoted in Hans Schaer, *op. cit.*, p. 19.
5. *The Church and Mental Health*, Paul Maves, ed. (New York: Charles Scribner's Sons, 1955), p. 45.

6. George Bernard Shaw, *Don Juan in Hell* (New York: Dodd, Mead & Company, 1951), p. 19.
7. *The Courage to Be* (New Haven: Yale University Press, 1952), p. 47.
8. *Ibid.*
9. Minou Drouet, *First Poems* (New York: Harper & Brothers, 1956), pp. 24, 25.
10. Robert B. McLeod, *Religious Perspectives in the Teaching of Experimental Psychology* (New Haven, Conn.: The Hazen Foundation, 1950).
11. *The Individual Psychology of Alfred Adler*, Heinz and Rowena Ansbacher, eds. (New York: Basic Books, Inc., 1956), p. 461. Used by permission of H. L. Ansbacher.
12. Viktor Frankl, *The Doctor and the Soul* (New York: Alfred A. Knopf, Inc., 1955), pp. 63, 67.
13. *Ibid.*, p. 71.
14. *Ibid.*, pp. 122-123.
15. II Corinthians 1:3-4.

CHAPTER 8. *The Psychology "Beyond Psychology"*

1. Gardner Murphy, *Personality: A Biosocial Approach to Origins and Structure* (New York: Harper & Brothers, 1947), p. 919f.
2. Otto Rank, *Beyond Psychology* (New York: Robert Brunner Books, Inc., 1941), pp. 1-16.
3. John Dewey, *A Common Faith* (New Haven: Yale University Press, 1934), p. 28.
4. Hans Schaer, *Religion and the Cure of Souls*

in Jung's Psychology (New York: Pantheon Books, Inc., 1950), p. 159.

5. Hans Schaer, *op. cit.*, p. 919.
6. Rank, *op. cit.*, p. 149.
7. *Ibid.*, p. 159.
8. *Ibid.*, p. 160.
9. *Ibid.*, p. 180.
10. *Ibid.*, pp. 192-193.
11. Talcott Parsons, *Religious Perspectives of College Teaching in Sociology and Social Psychology* (New Haven, Conn.: The Hazen Foundation, 1951), p. 44.
12. Rank, *op. cit.*, p. 61.
13. Robert B. McLeod, *Religious Perspectives in the Teaching of Experimental Psychology* (New Haven, Conn.: The Hazen Foundation, 1950), p. 12.
14. Emil Brunner, *The Christian Doctrine of Creation and Redemption: Dogmatics*, tr. by Olive Wyon (Philadelphia: Westminster Press, 1952), Vol. II, pp. 46-47.
15. Karl Barth, *Church Dogmatics*, tr. by A. C. Cochrane (Philadelphia: Westminster Press, 1953), Vol. III, p. 26.